Cambridge Elements

Elements in the Philosophy of Immanuel Kant
edited by
Desmond Hogan
Princeton University
Howard Williams
University of Cardiff
Allen Wood
Indiana University

KANT ON CITIZENSHIP AND POVERTY

Nicholas Vrousalis
Erasmus University Rotterdam

Shaftesbury Road, Cambridge CB2 8EA, United Kingdom

One Liberty Plaza, 20th Floor, New York, NY 10006, USA

477 Williamstown Road, Port Melbourne, VIC 3207, Australia

314–321, 3rd Floor, Plot 3, Splendor Forum, Jasola District Centre, New Delhi – 110025, India

Cambridge University Press is part of Cambridge University Press & Assessment, a department of the University of Cambridge.

We share the University's mission to contribute to society through the pursuit of education, learning and research at the highest international levels of excellence.

www.cambridge.org
Information on this title: www.cambridge.org/9781009671361

DOI: 10.1017/9781009671323

© Nicholas Vrousalis 2026

This publication is in copyright. Subject to statutory exception and to the provisions of relevant collective licensing agreements, with the exception of the Creative Commons version the link for which is provided below, no reproduction of any part may take place without the written permission of Cambridge University Press & Assessment.

An online version of this work is published at doi.org/10.1017/9781009671323 under a Creative Commons Open Access license CC-BY-NC-ND 4.0 which permits re-use, distribution and reproduction in any medium for non-commercial purposes providing appropriate credit to the original work is given. You may not distribute derivative works without permission. To view a copy of this license, visit https://creativecommons.org/licenses/by-nc-nd/4.0

When citing this work, please include a reference to the DOI 10.1017/9781009671323

First published 2026

A catalogue record for this publication is available from the British Library

ISBN 978-1-009-67136-1 Hardback
ISBN 978-1-009-67135-4 Paperback
ISSN 2397-9461 (online)
ISSN 2514-3824 (print)

Cambridge University Press & Assessment has no responsibility for the persistence or accuracy of URLs for external or third-party internet websites referred to in this publication and does not guarantee that any content on such websites is, or will remain, accurate or appropriate.

For EU product safety concerns, contact us at Calle de José Abascal, 56, 1°, 28003 Madrid, Spain, or email eugpsr@cambridge.org

Kant on Citizenship and Poverty

Elements in the Philosophy of Immanuel Kant

DOI: 10.1017/9781009671323
First published online: January 2026

Nicholas Vrousalis
Erasmus University Rotterdam
Author for correspondence: Nicholas Vrousalis, vrousalis@esphil.eur.nl

Abstract: According to Immanuel Kant, citizenship amounts to freedom (Freiheit), equality (Gleichheit), and civil self-sufficiency (Selbständigkeit). This Element provides a unifying interpretation of these three elements. I argue that Kant affirms the idea of interdependent independence: in the just society, citizens have independent use of their interdependent rightful powers. Kant therefore thinks of the modern state as a system of cooperative production, in which reciprocal entitlements to one another's labour carry a justificatory burden. The empirical form of that ideal is a republic of economically independent commodity producers. It follows that citizenship and poverty, for Kant, are inextricably connected. This shows how Kant's arguments anticipate Hegel's discussion of the division of labour, Marx's account of alienated labour, and Rawls' defence of a well-ordered society. This Element is also available as Open Access on Cambridge Core.

Keywords: Immanuel Kant, Karl Marx, GWF Hegel, John Rawls, distributive justice

© Nicholas Vrousalis 2026

ISBNs: 9781009671361 (HB), 9781009671354 (PB), 9781009671323 (OC)
ISSNs: 2397-9461 (online), 2514-3824 (print)

Contents

1 Introduction   1

2 Interdependent Independence: An Interpretation and Defence   3

3 Kantian Independence beyond Liberalism   29

4 From Independence to Economic Democracy   45

5 Conclusion   55

   References   57

1 Introduction

The French revolutionaries thought of human emancipation in a triptych, as freedom, equality, and fraternity. These could be three distinct values or three facets of the same value. Immanuel Kant holds the latter view. For Kant, the revolutionary triptych represents three facets of the unconditional value of humanity as an end in itself. Kant's political philosophy couches this representation in terms of an innate, pre-institutional right to freedom possessed by all humans as such. All other political rights and values are supposed to follow from that right. But Kant also emends the *content* of the revolutionary triptych. Citizenship, he argues, amounts to freedom (*Freiheit*), equality (*Gleichheit*), and civil self-sufficiency (*Selbständigkeit*). The first two attributes amount to freely consenting equals before the law. The interpretative question is what the third attribute adds to the first two: what does civil self-sufficiency add to free consent by equal juridical subjects?

This Element provides a unifying interpretation of Kant's theory of citizenship that responds to this question. I argue that *Selbständigkeit* contributes the idea of *interdependent independence*: the citizens' use of their interdependent rightful powers independently of the private choices of each. Kant's citizens are independent in the contrastive sense that their private choices do not depend on someone else's. But that does not make them independent of society, like the proverbial noble savage. Kantian independence does not amount to self-mastery – dependence *only* on one's own choices. Rather, I will argue that Kant's account of independence presupposes the interdependence of free and equal people through a *public* power, which enables each person to act independently of the *private* choices of others.

I will begin by showing that Kant's account of interdependence presupposes a social division of labour. The rightful condition, on Kant's view, involves free and equal people cooperating on the basis of reciprocally acceptable justifications. They thereby serve each other as equals, not as *servants*. Differently stated, the independence of free and equal people presupposes their 'self-standing' ability to exercise their civil rights. And this, in turn, presupposes that each control her share of society's productive assets. So citizenship and poverty, as mediated by the social division of labour, are inextricably connected.

A corollary of my interpretation is that poverty and wage-labour are not, in Kant's mind, justifiable forms of social standing. This is because no justification can be offered to former serfs or nascent proletarians for being servants of lords or of capitalists, respectively. So Kant's bigger picture sees the modern state as a system of cooperative production, in which the producers rightfully possess certain (productive) powers, whose interdependent exercise independently of private permission matters for justice. The empirical form of Kant's ideal is a republic of independent commodity producers. I will then show that this reading of *Selbständigkeit* can consistently explain Kant's disenfranchisement of women, wage labourers, and landless farmers; that it offers a robust alternative to influential Neoroman, libertarian, and proprietarian interpretations of the Kantian state; and that it can buttress an original account of community as productive interdependence. I will also explain how it anticipates Hegel's discussion of the division of labour, Marx's account of commodity fetishism and alienated labour, and Rawls theory of the well-ordered society.

This straight line from Kant to Marx begins with Rousseau, who takes the undifferentiated unity of the ancient democratic republics to be both infeasible and undesirable. The division of labour, Rousseau reasons, has forever put social undifferentiation behind. But he is concerned that the division of labour and the concomitant proliferation of private property might sow political disunity. His solution in the *Social Contract* is to subsume the economically induced differentiation under the unity of the general will (Rousseau 1973). That discussion presupposes a distinction between sovereignty and government. The former preserves political *unity* by creating general laws, while the latter preserves social *differentiation* by interpreting and applying these laws. Kant keeps the dualist structure of Rousseau's argumentation but adds a systematic derivation of Rousseau's conclusions from the point of view of the innate right of humanity.[1] This systematization, Kant thinks, preserves the differentiation of free and equal people without giving in to the disunity sown by private property and the division of labour.

In defending this interpretation, my textual focus throughout will be on Kant's mature theory of Public Right – his theory of the state. This theory features a constant tension between citizenship and property. To anticipate the argument slightly, I note that Kant's theory of the state needs citizenship to justify private property and not vice versa. His idea of 'provisional' acquired rights to external things, anticipating the rightful condition, would be superfluous without an independent account of that condition. Kant therefore needs an account of free and equal citizenship to determine which acquired rights are conclusive. As I explain in Section 2, his Rousseavian theory of sovereignty provides that account. But Kant's own description of independence covertly reintroduces property as a condition for citizenship. So we are stuck in a vicious circle between citizenship and property. This circle was etched into Rousseau's original distinction between the *bourgeois* and the citizen, eventually criticized by Marx in his essay on the Jewish question. Kant suggests a few ways out of

---

[1] For Kant's debts to Rousseau, see Colletti (1972) and Allison (2020).

this circle, the most convincing of which provides an account of *general injustice* that extends beyond the private rights of individuals. As I explain in Section 3, Rousseau's related idea that political equality is insufficient for *social* equality pervades Kant's political writings, as does the idea that social equality requires more than universal property.

The rest of this Element is structured as follows. Section 2 discusses alternative interpretations of Kant's theory of citizenship, from Sieyès to Arthur Ripstein. I argue that only interdependent independence, with its emphasis on independent use of one's interdependent powers, makes sense of Kant's own examples and contrasts. Section 3 extends these ideas to Kant's discussion of citizenship and poverty by criticizing an influential 'Toronto School' interpretation of that relationship. Interdependent independence does a better job, I argue, accounting for Kant's examples and contrasts. In passing, I will explain what this means for Kant's treatment of race and gender, for global justice, and for Kant's influence on Hegel and Marx. Section 4 explains how interdependent independence can help us make sense of contemporary debates in political philosophy. A Kant-inspired reading of citizenship offers a plausible and strictly egalitarian reading of Rawls' difference principle, which anticipates arguments for property-owning democracy and for public ownership of productive assets. The overall emerging picture is of Kant as a social democrat before it was cool.

2 Interdependent Independence: An Interpretation and Defence

Kant's theory of citizenship replaces the French revolutionary triptych of liberty, equality, and fraternity with freedom (*Freiheit*), equality (*Gleichheit*), and civil self-sufficiency (*Selbständigkeit*). The interpretative question is what the third attribute adds to the first two – what does self-sufficiency add to free consent by juridical equals? This section argues that *Selbständigkeit* adds the idea of *interdependent independence*: the independent possession and use of citizens' interdependent rightful powers.

I proceed as follows. In the first two sections I introduce Kant's theory of property, followed by his theory of citizenship. I then broach the idea of interdependent independence. This describes how members of a just state independently exercise their interdependent rightful powers. Kant's citizens, I argue, have as their object of legislation their own independence in productive community with others. As Kant sees it, franchise follows independence and not vice versa. I then explain why this inclusive interpretation of *Selbständigkeit* is exegetically superior to competing republican accounts, which attempt to explain Kant's exclusions by appeal to voter dispositions. I also show that, *pace* proprietarian and libertarian readings of Kant, his concern with property and propertylessness is derivative of a more fundamental concern with the independent exercise of the citizens' interdependent rightful powers.

2.1 Kant on Property

Kant's political philosophy is an attempt to deduce the idea of the liberal state from a single, pre-institutional, 'innate' right to freedom as independence (*Unabhängigkeit*) from the constraining choices of others (*DR* 6: 237).[2] A liberal state, for Kant, minimally includes the panoply of coercively enforceable individual rights, from the basic liberties (freedom of speech, conscience), through property rights in external things, to a welfare state (providing equality of opportunity and poverty relief). Kant's deduction of the liberal state has two movements. The first movement, Private Right, proceeds from a premiss about the innate right[3] of independence, to the justification of a provisional set of property rights (*DR* 6: 261 f.). This is a move from innate right to private property as its condition of possibility. But Kant also thinks that in the absence of a universally legislating public power, these private rights are indeterminate, nonbinding, and unenforceable.[4] The second movement, Public Right, is designed to correct these defects in the state of nature: enter omnilateral rule by a 'powerful and united will' that creates, interprets, and enforces law (*DR* 6:312ff). This establishes a 'rightful condition' under universal laws of right.[5] I will discuss the first movement in this section and the second in the next.

The first movement of *DR* is a movement from the innate right of humanity to private right.[6] In *DR*, Kant defines private property as follows:

> Mine is whatever I (according to the law of external freedom) bring within my possession, and what I (according to the postulate of practical reason)

---

[2] References are to *The Cambridge Edition of the Works of Immanuel Kant* (Cambridge: Cambridge University Press, 1992). Abbreviations are as follows: CPR=*Critique of Pure Reason;* CPJ=*Critique of the Power of Judgment;* CB=*Conjectural Beginning of Human History;* G=*Groundwork of the Metaphysics of Morals;* MM=*Metaphysics of Morals;* DR=*Doctrine of Right;* TP=*On the Common Saying: That May Be True in Theory But It Is of No Use in Practice;* LDPP=*Lectures and Drafts on Political Philosophy*.

[3] Kant distinguishes between 'innate' and 'acquired right', rights possessed by nature versus rights possessed by virtue of exercise of positive agency, such as an individual action (*DR* 6: 237).

[4] See Ripstein (2009) for a recent reconstruction along these lines and Flikschuh (2021) for a contrasting interpretation.

[5] It is important that this view is about the *external* freedom of persons and therefore not about the form of their *internal* motivation or maxims. Merely rightful obligations, for Kant, are externally individuated. It follows that Kant's political philosophy is orthogonal to his *ethics*: you can accept the former without accepting the latter. And that's a boon for the theory, because it does not depend on any comprehensive views about morality or the good life.

[6] Private Right is subdivided into three categories: property, contract, and status. I discuss status in Section 3.4.

have the capacity to use as an object of my will and, finally what I will should be mine (in accordance with the idea of a possibly united will). (DR 6: 258; see also 6: 267 f)

This section disentangles these three moments of Kant's concept of property: *possession*, *capacity*, and *will*, respectively. Each moment justifies a particular relation between a person and a thing. Kant establishes the first moment through his 'Universal Principle of Right', the second through a 'postulate of practical reason', and the third through the idea of 'provisional right'. Taken together, these three moments make up his theory of property. This theory not only rejects Locke's idea of a natural right to private property but also offers a structurally egalitarian, broadly Rousseauvian, account of property.

I begin with what Kant calls 'possession ... (according to the law of external freedom)'. Possession, in general, is the 'subjective condition of the possibility of the use of an object' (DR 6: 245). My possession of a thing is *rightful* if anyone's interfering with it without my consent would wrong me. That wrong, for Kant, is tantamount to a violation of my freedom as independence from the constraining choices of others (DR 6: 237).[7] This innate right to independence, Kant thinks, follows analytically from the

> Universal Principle of Right (UPR): Any action is right if it can coexist with anyone's freedom in accordance with a universal law, or if on its maxim the freedom of choice of each can coexist with everyone's freedom in accordance with a universal law. (DR 6: 230)

Right, for Kant, is connected with the 'authorization to use coercion' (6: 231). So to have rightful possession of some external object is to be able to coercively exclude others, *by right*, from using it. Note that Kant thinks that the UPR only establishes innate, not acquired, right: the possibility of rightful occupation of spaces, of rightful performance of basic actions, and of the holding of things. Consider what this means for possession. Suppose that, by the UPR, I can rightfully raise my arm. This means that I can also rightfully raise an apple *by holding it*. This set of authorizations, Kant thinks, is all contained in my innate right to independence. The problem is that innate right does not explain how I can rightfully perform the extended action of using the apple *without* holding it. Extending authorization from held to unheld things is the task of Kant's theory of property.

To clarify this crucial distinction, Kant draws from his Critical discussion of the *analytic* and the *synthetic a priori*. Consider your taking an apple from my hand without my consent. This wrongs me – it constitutes *battery*. The wrong, Kant thinks, follows analytically from my innate right. Contrast your taking,

---

[7] I here follow Baynes (1989).

without my consent, an apple which I own but I am not currently holding. This also wrongs me – it constitutes *theft*. But this violation does not follow *analytically* from my innate right, says Kant. Once it lies beyond my body, the representation of the apple as mine becomes a representation distinct from the representation of the apple as belonging to my body. Kant thinks that this makes the former representation into an analytically distinct idea. So if these two distinct ideas (what he calls 'intelligible' and 'physical' possession) are to be connected *a priori*, they must be connected *synthetically*. This, Kant says, requires a 'deduction' (*DR* 6: 250). The deduction must show that I can rightfully use the apple without holding it, or, equivalently, that there are freedom-consistent, coercively exclusionary apple-uses. So far, most Kant interpreters agree. Things get considerably more complicated once we turn to the details of Kant's deduction.[8]

The second moment in Kant's theory of property attempts to deduce a rightful capacity to use external things. Kant thinks this is established by the

> Postulate of practical reason with regard to rights (Postulate): It is possible for me to have any external object of my choice as mine, that, a maxim by which, if it were to become a law, an object of choice would in *itself* (objectively) have to *belong to no one (res nullius)* is contrary to rights. (DR 6: 250)

That the Postulate requires a proof, or at least an elaboration, transpires from the structure of Kant's argument (DR 6:250). I will assume, following recent Kant scholarship,[9] that the Postulate seeks to establish *dominion*, that is, a set of complete and enforceable property rights, including use, benefit, and alienation of external objects of choice (e.g. DR 6: 270). Even so, Kant's proof of the Postulate is obscure[10] and seems question-begging.[11] Here is one non-question-begging interpretation. Suppose I set the end of making a fruit salad. I am rightfully holding the apple in one hand and the pear in the other. Suppose that, in laying down the apple to chop the pear, I thereby lose title to the apple. This makes the rightful pursuit of the end of a fruit salad impossible, placing it into what Kant calls *res nullius*. But this leads to an inconsistency. Recall that independence requires that I be able to set and pursue ends independently of others. This includes fruit-salad-type ends. So I *must* be able to rightfully lay

---

[8] The *locus classicus* here is Ludwig (2005). [9] See, for example, Hasan and Stone (2022).
[10] Ripstein glosses it as follows: 'if you are physically capable of having means other than your person available to you for setting and pursuing purposes, consistent with the freedom of everyone, you can have a right to those means' (Ripstein 2009, 88). But consistency with everyone's freedom is what Kant is trying to prove.
[11] In his exposition on the Postulate, Kant *asserts* that there are freedom-consistent, exclusive formal uses of apples: 'in the use of things choice [is] formally consistent with everyone's outer freedom in accordance with universal laws' (DR 6: 250). This begs the question.

down the apple. Rightful 'intelligible' possession of the apple is therefore possible.

If this reconstruction is correct, then Kant's Postulate establishes that there *exist rightful uses of external things*. But we are not much the wiser, for this says nothing about *who* can own what. And this is what makes Kant's next move indispensable to his defence of private property. Kant writes that the Postulate

> can be called a permissive law of practical reason (*lex permissiva*), which gives us an authorization that could not be got from mere concepts of right as such, namely to put all others under an obligation, which they would not otherwise have, to refrain from using certain objects of our choice because we have been the first to take them into our possession. Reason wills that this hold as a principle, and it does this as practical reason, which extends itself a priori by this postulate of reason. (6:247)[12]

On the present reading, the permissive law turns the Postulate into an *agential* authorization: an authorization to those individuals with the relevant capacities to enlist external things in their pursuit of their own ends.[13] This makes certain things ownable. How do we go from ownability to ownership?

The final and crucial step in Kant's argument for private property is the possibility of a united will, or 'what I will should be mine (in accordance with the idea of a possibly united will)'. This is a Rousseauvian general-will-type authorization applied to external possession. Throughout *DR*, Kant insists on a distinction between

(a) 'common ownership' or the 'original community of land' (*Gemeinbesitz*) and
(b) 'private community' of private owners joining their properties together to form a 'collective possession (*Gesammtbesitz*)' (DR 6: 251; 267).

Kant criticizes the latter notion as presupposing contract and therefore private property. The former notion, by contrast, is an idea that 'has objective (rightfully practical) reality' and is connected *a priori* with the idea of the civil condition – the just state. Kant needs this connection with the civil condition

---

[12] There is much controversy as to the nature of permissive laws. Gregor (1986) and Hruschka (2004), as well as Hruschka and Byrd (2012), claim it is a function from indifferent actions – actions neither prohibited nor obligatory – to permissible actions: authorizations to exclusionary uses of external things through coercion. Others, like Tierney (2001) and Ypi (2014), take it to be a function from *prohibited* to permissible actions. I here follow Byrd and Hruschka's interpretation.

[13] In a nutshell, if x is rightfully formally usable and Rx is some rightful formal use of x, then the existence of a physical power whose *exercise* would constitute Rx makes x ownable. So if I have that physical power in the form of its possible exercise Rx and I exercise it to 'bring x under my control', then x is provisionally mine.

because he explicitly denies that there are innate or natural rights to property. He also mocks any Lockean appeal to labour-mixing as the ground of property acquisition (DR 6: 260 f). If Kant is right, then nothing can be nobody's in the state of nature. That is, if there are no natural rights to property, then nothing can belong to *nobody* by natural right, just as nothing can belong to somebody. But Kant does think that we can make sense of the idea of external things belonging jointly to *all* – things that can be used only with everyone else's permission. He reasons that to make something mine is *to withdraw it from the community by the hypothetical permission of all*.[14]

Baynes sums up this argument as follows:

> Rights and obligations can only arise through agreement, but a united agreement to recognize the right of original acquisition would be inconceivable unless everyone already possessed a prior claim to the land. Nor, of course, can this prior claim itself be based on a still earlier agreement. Since persons and between persons-relations are based on agreements between persons – relations between persons and things – if the land was not originally owned by someone no property rights could ever arise. The conclusion drawn ... is that the notion of an original, non-contractual common ownership is a necessary presupposition for the possibility of property rights; without it no obligations regarding property could arise, including the most basic obligation to enter into a civil society. (Baynes 1989, 441)

There is some consensus among Kant scholars that this 'obligation' is a natural duty to support just institutions. On this interpretation, the structure of Kantian property rights must *anticipate* the structure of the just state. Rafeeq Hasan, for example, argues that in the 'state of nature property claims do not wrong others, but anticipate a condition in which the authority to make such claims can no longer be unilaterally determined' (Hasan 2017, 850; see also Guyer 1996). It follows that the authority to make private property claims in the state of nature is dependent on the structure of the rightful condition which the state of nature ought to anticipate.

Now return to this passage:

> Mine is whatever I (according to the law of external freedom) bring within my possession, and what I (according to the postulate of practical reason) have the capacity to use as an object of my will and, finally what I will should be mine (in accordance with the idea of a possibly united will). (6: 258; see also 6: 268 f)

---

[14] It is significant that here Kant is not discussing *disjunctive* possession: occupation of the space and holding of the things I happen to occupy and hold. Kant does say that 'All people are originally (that is, before all juridical acts of the will) in legitimate possession of the land, that is, they have a right to be where Nature or chance (without their choice) has placed them' (DR 6: 262). But this does not explain the pervasiveness of his references to original communal possession.

Kant on Citizenship and Poverty

I have broken this down as follows. For any external object of choice, x, the 'law of external freedom' says that x is ownable. This moment of 'possession' says nothing about who owns what, not even provisionally. This indeterminacy is resolved by the Postulate, read as a permissive law. The Postulate says that there are *agents* who can own x. These agents receive an authorization, or normative power they would not otherwise have, which puts others under an obligation not to interfere with their exclusive uses of x. But this is not to say who owns what, even provisionally. To establish provisional ownership, I must 'will' that x be mine, subject to that willing *anticipating* a rightful condition. In anticipating, I am to ask whether everyone could hypothetically permit me to withdraw x from communal use. Then, and only then, is x mine. So Kant not only rejects natural rights to private property but also derives property from an idea of original communal possession. Kant de-Lockeanizes property theory by Rousseauvifying it.

So much for summarizing Kant's theory of property. I now discuss the second movement of Kant's argument for the liberal state, from Private to Public Right. Its central feature is a theory of citizenship.

2.2 Kant on Citizenship

Citizenship plays a crucial role in Kant's second justificatory step for a liberal state (see *TP* 8: 290–297 and *DR* 6: 314–316). In *DR* §46, Kant again opens with a Rousseauvian argument about the unity of sovereign power. He argues that the state's legislative authority belongs to 'the concurring and united will of all,' where 'each decides the same thing for all and all for each'. He adds that, since one 'can never do wrong in what he decides upon with regard to himself', it follows that the legislation of such a united will must be consistent with the demands of right. But who are Kant's co-legislators?

Kant's co-legislating citizen has three normative attributes (*rechtliche ... Attribute*): he[15] enjoys freedom (*Freiheit*), 'the attribute of obeying no other law than that to which he has given his consent'; equality (*Gleichheit*), the attribute of 'not recognizing among the people any superior with the moral capacity to bind him as a matter of right in a way that he could not in turn bind

---

[15] For Kant a citizen is, invariably, a 'he'. *DR* contrasts with *TP* in that the former does not ascribe to women a naturalized property of being unfit to vote. Rather, in *DR*, Kant seems to be saying that women are dependent just by dint of extant social conditions. See J. Weinrib (2008) for a defence of this interpretation, Kleingeld (1993) for an influential discussion of Kant's sexism, and Section 3.4 for a discussion of the gendered division of labour.

the other'; and civil self-sufficiency (*Selbständigkeit*),[16] the attribute of 'owing his existence and preservation to his own rights and powers as a member of the commonwealth, not to the choice of another among the people' (*DR* 6:314). Freedom, equality, and civil self-sufficiency, then, are the ideal public expression of Kantian independence. What remains to be explained is what the third attribute adds to the first two.

A preliminary explanation follows Kant's account of the franchise. After suggesting that 'the only qualification for being a citizen' is 'being fit to vote', Kant adds that this

> [P]resupposes the self-sufficiency of someone who, as one of the people, wants to be not just a part (*Teil*) of the commonwealth but also a member (*Glied*) of it, that is, a part of the commonwealth acting from his own choice in community (*Gemeinschaft*) with others. The quality of being self-sufficient, however, requires a distinction between active and passive citizens, though the concept of a passive citizen seems to contradict the concept of a citizen as such. The following examples can serve to remove this difficulty: an apprentice in the service of a merchant or artisan; a domestic servant (as distinguished from a civil servant); a minor; all women and, in general, anyone whose preservation in existence (his being fed and protected) depends not on his management of his own business but on arrangements made by another (except the state). All these people lack civil personality and their existence is, as it were, only inherence (*Inhärenz*). (*DR* 6: 314; translation amended)

Kant's passive citizens[17] enjoy freedom and equality if they possess legal standing as parts ($\neq$ members) of the commonwealth and if they can work their 'way up from this passive condition to an active one' (*DR* 6: 315). Both conditions are satisfied, Kant implies, in the case of apprentices, domestic servants, minors, and women, albeit *passively*. Minors, for example, enjoy a right 'to the care of their parents until they are able to look after themselves' (*DR* 6: 280), a right entailed by their innate right to independence. It follows that enjoyment of innate right is compatible with de facto lack of control over its active exercise. On the interpretation I will present, Kant purports to justify this lack of control by the dependent nature of the right-holder's labour. Civil

---

[16] Mary Gregor renders both *Unabhängigkeit* (as a feature of the innate right to freedom) and *bürgerlichen Selbständigkeit* (as a feature of civil status) as 'independence', using the 'civil' operator to distinguish the latter from the former. On the interpretation I will present, Kant uses *Unabhängigkeit* to refer to the content of right, whereas *Selbständigkeit*, along with freedom and equality, are the complete public expression of that content. In keeping with recent scholarship, I render *Selbständigkeit* as 'self-sufficiency'.

[17] There is some evidence that Kant borrows the distinction between active and passive citizens from the French constitution of 1791 and the writings of Sieyès (Maliks 2014; Davies 2020). In Section 2.5, I will show that Kant's interpretation of the distinction differs from Sieyès' in crucial respects.

self-sufficiency, on this view, establishes a presumption for independent use of your rightful powers, including your productive powers. If I am right, then self-legislating citizens in the Kantian state must enjoy interdependent independence, that is, the ability to make their own (productive) choices independently of the private choices of others. I now explain the relevance of this interpretation.

My interpretation of civil self-sufficiency is key to understanding Kant's disenfranchisement not only of apprentices, domestic servants, women, and minors – all of whom are subject to fiduciary 'status' relationships – but also of wage labourers and landless farmers – who are not. In the *DR* passage immediately following the definition of civil self-sufficiency (see the quotation above), Kant writes:

> The woodcutter I hire to work in my yard; the blacksmith in India, who goes into people's houses to work on iron with his hammer, anvil and bellows, as compared with the European carpenter or blacksmith who can put the products of his work up as goods for sale to the public; the private tutor, as compared with the school teacher; the tenant farmer as compared with the leasehold farmer, and so forth; these are mere underlings of the commonwealth because they have to be under the direction or protection of other individuals, and so do not possess civil self-sufficiency. (*DR* 6: 314–315; translation amended)

The Indian travelling blacksmith[18] contrasts with those subject to status relations, in that she is merely contractually bound to 'let and hire' her productive powers to her employer(s) (*DR* 6: 285).[19] But the blacksmith's position is similar to those subject to status relationships in that she, too, lacks civil self-sufficiency. According to Kant, the Indian blacksmith enjoys freedom and equality insofar as she *could* come to own enough iron and thereby come to bind her employer to as much as the employer actually binds her. This is the significance of Kant's *equal opportunity proviso*, that 'anyone can work his way up from this passive condition to an active one' (*DR* 6: 315). But the blacksmith presently lacks iron ownership, which means she lacks independent use of her productive powers. In order to exercise these powers, she must get permission from the iron owner(s) to use the iron they own, which means she must put her powers at their disposal. She therefore lacks civil self-sufficiency. Like the minor, the Indian blacksmith remains subject 'to the

---

[18] Moran (2021, 4) discusses the origins of Kant's example.
[19] The labour contract normally counts as a status relation, what Kant calls *locatio (conductio) personae*. This is the 'granting of my powers to a principal as her agent in return for payment'. The Indian blacksmith case seems to involve not a labour contract, but rather 'granting another the use of my powers for a specified price'. Kant classifies this as *locatio operae* (*DR* 6:285). The argument that follows applies to both sets of cases.

choice of another among the people' (*DR* 6: 314),[20] quite independently of a supervening status relationship.

The rest of this section argues for three claims. First, *Selbständigkeit* is the idea that free and equal people can co-legislate if and only if they have independent use of their rightful powers as members of the commonwealth. Absent such independence, dependent producers cannot legislate on behalf of their own agency. Second, the relationship between citizenship and property, for Kant, does not have the educational, psychological, or anti-corruption significance it has for Sieyès, for the French constitution of 1791, or for contemporary neo-Roman interpretations of citizenship.[21] Rather, property is relevant only insofar as it gives citizens unsubjected formal discretion over the exercise of their rightful powers. By enjoying such discretion, Kant's interdependent citizens independently facilitate the conditions of their mutual independence. Third, Kant takes the empirical form of independence in the modern state to be independent commodity production.[22] That is, Kant's citizen uses her productive powers to produce external means for others, without having to make her powers into their means. So, in depending only on the *content* of exchange relationships – what she produces with her own powers – each member of the commonwealth depends only on her own 'ability, industry, and good fortune' (*TP* 8:296). After introducing the interdependent independence interpretation, I will defend each of these claims in what follows.

2.3 Citizenship and *Selbständigkeit*

Here's a reconstruction of *DR* §46, Kant's main discussion of citizenship. This reconstruction must explain why, for Kant, the franchise follows economic independence and not vice versa. More precisely, economic dependence suffices to disenfranchise dependents in fiduciary status relationships – e.g. the minor and the domestic servant – *and* non-fiduciary contractual relationships – e.g. the Indian blacksmith. The structure of this interpretation is as follows (Kant on the left column, my reconstruction on the right):

---

[20] Kant's active/passive distinction immediately recalls language users and smokers. An active language user, for example, is dependent for the exercise of her linguistic powers on the language or linguistic community as a whole. But, unlike the passive user, she is not dependent on any particular language user for the exercise of that power – the production of linguistic meaning. If the social generation of linguistic meaning was the only feature of human interaction, then Kantian independence would only be about subjection in the give and take of linguistic representations. But humans are spatiotemporally located embodied beings, who can make things other than words into their means. They can make their own bodies, the bodies of others, as well as nonhuman animals and objects into their means. All of these facts are, for Kant, assimilable into a non-empirical argument for the rightful condition.

[21] See, for example, Skinner (1997).

[22] On the distinction between ideal and empirical forms of independence, see Patellis (2013).

'[O]nly the united will of all, insofar as each decides the same thing for all and all for each ... can be legislative.' (*DR* 6: 314)	(1) The legislating united will of all involves each deciding for all and all for each, such that each legislator legislates for herself.
'[W]hen someone makes arrangements about another, it is always possible for him to do the other wrong; but he can never do wrong in what he decides upon with regard to himself.' (*DR* 6: 313–14)	(2) A will legislating for herself cannot wrong others (in that legislative capacity). All right proceeds from such a will only.
	So
	(3) The united will's co-legislators cannot wrong each other (in that legislative capacity), such that all right proceeds from their united will only. (from 1, 2)
'The only qualification for being a citizen is being fit to vote ... [T]he attributes of a citizen are: lawful freedom, ... civil equality, ... and civil self-sufficiency ... ' (*DR* 6: 314)	(4) One is a co-legislator, and therefore fit to vote, if and only if she is a citizen possessing the attributes of freedom, equality, and civil self-sufficiency.
	So
	(5) Only citizens possessing these attributes ('active citizens') can legislate rightfully (in their legislative capacities), such that all right proceeds from their united will only. (from 3, 4)
'[T]he blacksmith in India ... ha[s] to be under the direction or protection of other individuals, and so do[es] not possess civil self-sufficiency.' (*DR* 6: 315)	(6) The Indian blacksmith lacks civil self-sufficiency.
	So
	(7) The Indian blacksmith is not fit to vote. (from 4, 6)

In a nutshell, Kant could not have thought that dependents should be disenfranshised, unless he thought that, in legislating, they would be making 'arrangements about another'. Economically dependent citizens, for example, would be legislating not for *themselves* as independent citizens, but only for their propertied masters as citizens. But then, Kant reasons, those dependents cannot possibly legislate rightfully. The interpretative challenge consists in offering an account of *Selbständigkeit* broad enough to explain why the dependent cannot legislate (claim (5)) and why *that* suffices for their disenfranchisement (claim (7)).

The only interpretation that makes these inferences exegetically palatable, I now argue, is the *interdependent independence interpretation of civil self-sufficiency* (hereafter: *interdependent independence*).[23] This interpretation establishes a presumption in favour of enjoying unsubjected exercise of your rights and powers, including your productive powers,[24] as a member of the commonwealth. Interdependent independence sees legitimate public power as regulating the compossible choice sets of interdependent choosers. These choosers (re)produce their own lives by exercising their commonwealth-conferred rights and (productive) powers independently of the private choices of others. Here is some further textual evidence for this reconstruction.

DR §46 calls the active citizen a 'member' (*Glied*). This contrasts with the passive citizen, a mere 'part' (*Teil*) of the state. Kant suggests that the choices of active citizens form a community (*Gemeinschaft*) and that the concomitant status of passive citizens is 'as it were, mere inherence' (*Inhärenz*). These terms are explicitly connected in Kant's Critical philosophy. In the *Critique of Pure Reason* Kant contrasts the reciprocal determination of 'coordinated relations' (as in members of a body) with the 'subordinated' relation of effect to cause. The former relation, unlike the latter, constitutes a community (*Gemeinschaft*) between 'agent and patient' (*CPR* A80/B106). Inherence, on the other hand, is contrasted with subsistence, in that only subsistent entities – substances – have causal powers. It follows that only substances can partake of

---

[23] Of the four possibilities: non-interdependent dependence, non-interdependent independence, interdependent dependence, and interdependent independence, the first is incoherent. Kant follows Rousseau in thinking that, of the last three, only interdependent independence counts as human freedom proper. I contrast non-interdependent and interdependent independence in Section 2.5.

[24] A productive power is a non-normative ability to bring about an effect by making a physical object into a means to that effect. I possess a productive power when I can cook an omelette in my kitchen; I also possess that power when I can cook an omelette at the cookshop under a division of labour with other omelette producers. A productive power contrasts with a *productive choice*, which is intentional exercise of a productive power.

community: they are *independent* as substances but *interdependent* as reciprocally dependent on other substances.²⁵

Kant applies these categories explicitly to politics in the *Critique of the Power of Judgment*. In a footnote discussing the French Revolution, he applies the idea of organization to the 'body politic' and suggests that 'in such a whole, each member (*Glied*) should certainly be not merely a means but at the same time an end ... whose position and function should be determined by the idea of the whole' (*CPJ* 5: 375). On the present interpretation, political community is a form of reciprocal interdependence through the social division of labour. The 'body politic' is the united will of independent 'substances', that is, of free and equal people in independent possession and use of their rightful powers.

Now, the criteria for voter-fitness, on this view, are entailed by three *a priori* premisses (1, 2, 4). The first two (1, 2) reflect Kant's views of the appropriate object of legislation, namely the self-legislating will herself. Kant then identifies that will with free and equal people in independent possession and exercise of their rightful powers (4). It follows that the domestic servant, the private tutor, and the Indian blacksmith cannot legislate. For in legislating, they would not be *self*-legislating: their agency, as 'inhering' in the agency of others, cannot be exercised in their own name. As I explain presently, none of these inferences makes sense unless Kant thinks of the rightful condition as a system of cooperative production, in which the subjection of labour capacity to a private will undermines one's formal standing to legislate universally.

I now offer a unifying explanation for these assertions, based on the idea of interdependent independence.

2.4 The Unifying Explanation: Interdependent Independence

Kant's disenfranchising exclusions are not, I now argue, about *how* citizens are disposed to vote. Rather, they are about the nature of the *object* of universal legislation in the Kantian state. The idea is that only interdependent independents can, in legislating, *self*-legislate, that is, make arrangements about their own agency.

Suppose the European and the Indian blacksmith share a qualitatively identical productive power of working iron into hammers. Both produce, say, an equal output per hour out of equal inputs; both serve the commonwealth by making it richer by some hammers. Suppose, further, that both enjoy the same set of

---

²⁵ In the 'Analogies of Experience' Kant argues that 'dynamic community', which he sometimes denotes as '*commercium*', is transcendentally necessary for the objective simultaneity of substances (*CPR* A211-215/B258-62).

commonwealth-conferred legal rights to exercise these productive powers, in addition to the right to own iron. They are therefore free and equal before the law. Kant implies that the Indian blacksmith owns no iron, such that, if she is to exercise her productive powers by working iron, she must ask permission from the iron owner(s).[26] The Indian blacksmith's ironlessness thereby gives the iron owner(s) discretion over the exercise of the blacksmith's productive powers – her ability to work iron into hammers. According to Kant, it follows that she lacks *Selbständigkeit*. That is, her labour process, and therefore *the condition of exercise of her commonwealth-conferred legal rights and powers*, is de facto unilaterally controlled by others.[27] This means that her legislative choices do not just affect what belongs to her: the Indian blacksmith is interdependent but not independent. Kant infers that she cannot legislate rightfully. In elaboration of this inference, consider an analogy with musical production.

Suppose you own the musical instrument I need in order to perform as a member of the orchestra. Then you can, by legal right, deprive me of it at will. It follows that I cannot exercise my music-making powers as an orchestra member by playing that instrument, except through your unilateral permission. This way my music-making, even if realized, serves two masters: you and the orchestra. I might, of course, be unaware of that. But that's irrelevant. Kant's objection is *not* that my dependence on you might make me fearful, obsequious or servile in my music-making, inclined to pursue your ends as opposed to mine, and so on. These empirically contingent effects on my psychology are not at the centre of Kant's democratic theory (which is why they are never mentioned).[28] Rather, the ground of my exclusion from orchestra membership *just is* the dependence of the realization of my music-making ends on your unilateral will. That is, even if I were to perform, my performance would still be conditional on your permission. And that would be true whether I know it or not. Such dependence, Kant thinks, normatively disqualifies me from making arrangements about my own music-making. This disqualifies me from occupying the office of music-maker altogether.

Contrast the case where I or the orchestra itself control(s) my instrument. Perhaps the orchestra has public rules meant to serve the goal of music-making: who can occupy the office of violinist, pianist, and cellist, who can use the instruments under what conditions, and so on. Then, in setting the instrument as

---

[26] Rafeeq Hasan elaborates: 'What the Indian blacksmith lacks is not the ability to use what is his: his tools and labor power. Rather, what he lacks is iron, that is, the raw materials, which he can transform through his productive activity into something of exchange value' (Hasan 2017, 921).

[27] Ripstein (2017, 211) argues that Kant's account of citizenship presupposes a distinction between the possession- and exercise-conditions of political rights, but does not discuss human productive powers or the relevance of interdependence. See also James (2016).

[28] I criticize these broadly neo-Roman ideas in Section 2.5.

a means to the realization of my music-making powers, the *exercise* of these powers is subject to nothing but the end of music-making. I therefore no longer serve two masters; my agency is no longer alienated to you.[29] Now note that this independence does not preclude interdependence—in fact, the former presupposes the latter. As an orchestra member, I am dependent on you, just as you are on me, for *nothing but* the mutual exercise of our orchestra-conferred musical powers. That is, we are mutually dependent for doing out our respective parts in the division of musical labour. So the orchestra's powers are now only the musicians' interdependent musical powers, independently exercised.

Kantian *Selbständigkeit* supports this analogy between orchestra and modern state.[30] Take the European blacksmith, who produces means that others need in order to set and pursue their ends as members of that state. By selling the hammers she makes in return for wigs, cloth, or money, she exercises her productive power without having to 'alienate' it to others (*TP* 8: 295). That way, she produces means that facilitate the unsubjected purposiveness of the wigmaker or the tailor, without making her own purposiveness into their means. The European blacksmith thereby serves 'no one other than the commonwealth' (*TP* 8: 295), *the condition of her own independence*. The Indian blacksmith, by contrast, serves two masters: the commonwealth *and* her employer(s). For to alienate your productive powers is to serve a (series of) private master(s), rather than the conditions of your own freedom. So, even if the Indian blacksmith were deemed fit to vote by dint of her independent-mindedness, she would still be bound to making her productive powers into the means of others.[31] By interdependent independence, she would thereby lack the normative power to legislate on behalf of her own agency. Crucially, the nature of this disempowerment is independent of the Indian blacksmith's psychological dispositions or the contingent content of her material ends. Her

---

[29] The orchestra analogy carries no presumption that my dependence on your unilateral will threatens the *orchestra's* music-making powers. It is perfectly conceivable that, barring barriers to entry, there are enough musicians and instruments to allow the orchestra to exercise its powers regardless of what I do.

[30] The Kantian republic is unlike an orchestra, in that it has no *material* ends. Its sole end is the formal compossibility of the choices of all under universal laws of right, an end which justifies reciprocal coercion for its realization (*DR* 6: 231f). For the metaphysically non-mysterious implications of the orchestra analogy for liberal political morality, see Dworkin (2000, 225–230).

[31] That persons must *produce* their own independence, that is, set themselves means which might include material objects used by others, is no more a contingent fact than that human bodies can collide. More generally, persons are generically not just end-setters, but also means-setters. By creating laws, public offices and by engaging in Smithian 'truck, barter, and exchange', they authorize other persons to act in their name in pursuit of their own freedom. These claims, along with the idea that to have your powers under my unilateral discretion is to set *you* as a means, are all interdependent independence needs. In *DR* §46, Kant makes this set of a priori propositions into elements of a theory of citizenship.

disempowerment is only about the formal exercise of her own powers as subject to the private choices of others.[32]

The orchestra analogy can explain why Kant's democratic theory is progressive for his time (Maliks 2014; Weinrib 2008). Suppose that orchestra membership can be expanded in either of two ways: the orchestra itself provides more instruments to more musicians or more musicians bring their own instruments. Both arrangements allow for the free, unsubjected exercise of this extended membership's music-making powers.[33] In a similar vein, Kant proposes to extend independence – and therefore the franchise – by extending public poverty relief to 'those who are unable to maintain themselves' (*DR* 6: 326);[34] by enforcing the opportunity of anyone to 'work his way up from his active condition into an active one' (*DR* 6: 315);[35] and by giving *every* active citizen an equal vote. This egalitarianism of voting shares is most explicit in Kant's discussion of the estates. Having raised the question 'how it came about that many human beings who could otherwise have acquired a lasting status of possession were *thereby reduced merely to serving [the landowner] in order to be able to live*' (*TP* 8: 296, my emphasis), Kant explains that enfranchisement should depend only on the 'status of possession, not ... the size of ... possessions.' So possession matters because and insofar as it evinces independent use of one's powers, including her ability to feed and protect herself by right.[36] I will return to this in Section 2.5.

To sum up the argument so far: according to interdependent independence, an active citizen is someone whose exercise of her state-conferred rights and powers is not subject to another (set of) non-state agent(s), just as an independent musician is someone whose exercise of her orchestra-conferred musical powers is not subject to another (set of) non-orchestra agent(s). Kant's

---

[32] Kate Moran argues that an employment contract may constrain the blacksmith's normative ability to participate in politics. And since Kantian citizens, she argues, have a 'civic duty' of political participation, the Indian blacksmith cannot adequately discharge her duty as a citizen (Moran 2021, 18ff). Both claims seem plausible, but there is little evidence that Kant affirms them. Interdependent indepedence presupposes neither of these claims.

[33] A further important parallel between state membership and orchestra membership is that one cannot contract her way into either. Just as I cannot, by right, purchase eligibility for the office of violinist, likewise I cannot, by right, purchase eligibility for the office of citizenship. 'A citizen's right to vote is not a private power to be used for private purposes' (Ripstein 2009, 138).

[34] In *DR* 6:314, Kant suggests that your dependence on the state for 'being fed and protected' – as opposed to dependence on a unilateral will – does not make you a passive citizen.

[35] Kant does not consider structural constraints. The individual blacksmith, for example, can become self-employed, but *all* blacksmiths cannot simultaneously become self-employed under the capitalist mode of production. Cohen (1983) discusses conceptual issues arising from this distinction between freedom *in sensu diviso* and *in sensu composito*.

[36] Even in *TP*, which emphasizes property more strongly than *DR*, Kant adduces possession and property in order to contrast it with servitude and unilateral dependence on others. Inherited wealth, winning the lottery, and so on only confer independence insofar as they facilitate independent exercise of one's powers, including her productive powers.

schoolteacher and European blacksmith, for example, enjoy both (a) a set of commonwealth-conferred political powers and (b) unsubjected formal discretion over their conditions of exercise.[37] Kant's private tutor and Indian blacksmith, by contrast, enjoy (a) but not (b). Both must get permission to use their powers, which trivially entails that they lack discretion over their exercise. So the private tutor and the Indian blacksmith lack civil self-sufficiency. This, Kant thinks, suffices to disenfranchise them: *only the independent producers can, in legislating, legislate on behalf of their own rightful powers.*

Contemporary liberalism solves this problem by severing the link between franchise and independence, thereby enfranchising wage labour. But this move, which proceeds by denying the presupposition in premiss (4), misunderstands the spirit of Kant's argument. Kant wants to make independence – unsubjected exercise of one's interdependent rightful powers – central to political life in the modern state. The rightful condition must therefore reflect more than free consent by juridical equals. This is what *Selbständigkeit* adds to the *Freiheit-Gleichheit* diptych. And this is also why the Indian blacksmith, lacking *Selbständigkeit*, cannot self-legislate. The way Kant sees it, her productive dependence means she would not be legislating on behalf of her own freedom, *even if she had the right to vote.*[38]

I now argue that interdependent independence is the only consistent exegesis of Kantian citizenship. If I am right, then Kant's state does not just represent a republic of property owners united by state-enforced relations of property, contract, and status.[39] After all, this bucolic picture is compatible with a republic of *non*-interdependent subsistence farmers – something resembling a Jeffersonian agrarian republic. Kant's picture is different. For him, an omnilateral will represents a republic of free citizens enjoying *all-round interdependence* under conditions of independent use of their rightful powers. It is more port city than agrarian republic.

2.5 Against the Neo-Roman Interpretation

I have, so far, argued that Kant's active citizens enjoy, in addition to freedom and equality, interdependent independence. This third attribute, *Selbständigkeit*, establishes a presumption against alien unilateral control over the exercise of

---

[37] Insofar as the orchestra musician gets her instrument from the orchestra, she is not dependent on a private will for the exercise of her musical powers. The European blacksmith, by contrast, must find a market for her products. In *TP* and *DR*, Kant implies that market dependence, as such, does *not* preclude independence (contrast the *LDPP* passage quoted below).

[38] Marx would take up this contradiction between political and economic emancipation, as well as the corresponding distinction between citizen and *bourgeois*, in his essay on the Jewish question, half a century after Kant. The distinction's most recent incarnation is Rawls's (1971, 223ff) seminal discussion of the basic liberties and their fair value.

[39] This is the picture recently painted by Ripstein (2009).

their rightful powers, including their productive powers. This section rebuts a broadly neo-Roman interpretation of active citizenship.

Some philosophers take Kant's disenfranchising exclusions to depend on an empirical claim from cognitive, volitional, or motivational corruption. Luke Davies, for example, argues that, for Kant,

> those who depend on private relations of authority for their survival are more likely to act in a way that advances the private interests of themselves or those on whom they depend when participating in lawgiving. (Davies 2021, 23)

This *corruption reading* of Kant's exclusions resonates with Claus Dierksmeier's idea that 'having sovereignty over your own business and household would educate you to participate adequately in the affairs of political government and sovereignty' (Dierksmeier 2002, 50). In a similar vein, Jacob Weinrib cautions against the 'potentially particularizing' nature of the will of dependent persons, who cannot, by dint of that dependence, 'achieve the requisite level of impartiality to contribute to the general will' (Weinrib 2008, 11). Sarah Holtman underlines the possibility of 'fearful decisions of subordinates' in response to power over them, which she contrasts to 'the well-informed and skillful reasoning of those who comprehend and are committed to justice' (Holtman 2004, 100). And Rafeeq Hasan argues that 'Kant's ostensible point about the passive citizen is that . . . he is likely to *feel pressured* into voting the interests of his boss . . .' (Hasan 2017, 922, emphasis added).

These broadly neo-Roman concerns are not Kant's concerns: his account of civil self-sufficiency is not premised on a corruption idea. For one, Kant never mentions the psychological dispositions presupposed by such an idea. Furthermore, there is no reason to think that a disposition towards servility (Davies), partiality (Weinrib), or fearfulness (Holtman) will necessarily accompany the dependent.[40] Indeed, the independent might manifest these dispositions and to a greater extent. Finally, the corruption reading cannot explain why dependence makes rightful self-legislation impossible. Consider the following inference from the argument of Section 2.3:

> (5) Only citizens possessing the attributes [of freedom, equality, and civil self-sufficiency] can legislate rightfully.
> So (8) Citizens lacking these attributes cannot legislate rightfully.

---

[40] Nor is there any textual evidence that Kant's account is about the ways in which dependence on others hampers one's ability 'to exercise her judgment independently of others' (Davies 2021, 21) or makes them 'beholden to their economic patrons' (Wood 2014, 88). If the laws are enforced, as Kant assumes, then these patrons can only enforce the contractual obligations of dependents, not more than that.

There is no textual evidence in Kant that (8) refers to the *empirical dispositions* of voters. Kant offers no evidence that extending the franchise would make new voters fearful, obsequious, or motivationally less likely to legislate rightfully.[41] If anything, one would expect the opposite. These corruption readings therefore misunderstand the thrust of Kant's position, which follows validly from certain a priori claims about the proper object of political legislation and the nature of political community (claims 1, 2, 4). As *DR*§46 makes clear from the outset, Kant is interested in the *purely normative features* that define independence, as well as the accompanying non-psychological features of agents 'as members of the commonwealth'.[42]

Consider a further illuminating contrast. Kate Moran has recently traced the neo-Roman ideas underlying the corruption reading back to Sieyès and his discussion of the 'lackeys of feudalism' (Moran 2021, 9). In that discussion, Sieyès offers an argument for why 'women, children, and foreigners' should only be accounted as passive citizens, namely that they 'contribute nothing to the maintenance of the public establishment'.[43] Davies draws a suggestive parallel between this argument and an important passage from Kant's drafts:

> The possessors of land are the genuine state subjects because they depend on the land for *vitam sustinendo* [sustenance of life]. To the extent, however, that they farm only as much as they need to live they are not citizens of the state. For they could not contribute to the commonwealth. Only possessors of great amounts of land who have many servants, who themselves as servants cannot be citizens, could be citizens, and yet they are citizens only to the extent that their surplus is purchased by others who, as free citizens, do not depend on the land. But one must first have citizens before one have subjects of the state. Thus in regard to the commonwealth the *pactum civile* [civil contract] comes first, with the caveat that those whose existence depends on the will of another, thus those who do not enjoy a free existence, have no vote. (*LDPP* 23: 137–38; translation amended)

---

[41] This objection also afflicts Honneth's (2024) attempt to argue for the regulation of labour on the basis of 'democratic participation'. The empirical question whether the capitalist organization and content of labour undermines democratic participation is orthogonal to the non-empirical question whether it wrongs the workers and citizens as such.

[42] Again, this is not to consider agents as psychologically or dispositionally rich social subjects, such that voter fitness is not an epistemic, cognitive, or motivational disposition. Moran (2021) makes a compelling case that these passages do not support *any* material reading of the relevant inequalities (whether in wealth, cognitive, or volitional capacities). She also argues that Kant's pivotal example of the Indian blacksmith involves merely formal, as opposed to material, inequality.

[43] Cited in Davies (2020, 17).

Pace Davies,[44] this passage refutes the Sieyès reading. For consider: Kant's surplus-producing landowners can certainly contribute to taxation or to 'the maintenance of the public establishment'. So, by Sieyès' reading of 'contribution', these landowners should be enfranchised. Yet Kant *disenfranchises* them ('... and yet they are citizens only to the extent ...'). Why? Because 'contribution', for Kant, means something more specific than it does for Sieyès, namely independent labour contribution: participation in a division of labour among juridical equals with independent use of their (productive) powers. How else are we to explain Kant's argument that *only those landowners who produce a surplus consumed by nonlandowners* (those who 'do not depend on the land') can be citizens? Since Kant's landowners do not partake of that interdependence, they are, just for that reason, disenfranchised.

Unlike the neo-Roman reading, interdependent independence illuminates both sets of contrasts implied by the *LDPP* passage. First, civil self-sufficiency contrasts with the *non*-civil self-sufficiency of the subsistence farmer and the surplus-producing landowner who only sells to other landowners.[45] Second, it contrasts with the civil *non*-self-sufficiency of servants and wage labourers. The first group enjoy independence, but are not interdependent; the second group enjoy interdependence but are not independent. The European blacksmith, by contrast, enjoys both. She enjoys interdependence by selling the product of the exercise of her powers in the market. And she enjoys independence by not having to make her productive powers into the means of others. She thereby acts from her 'own choice in community with others' (*DR* 6: 314). In the terms of the Critical philosophy, she is a 'substance' in 'community' with all other 'substances' of the 'body politic'. This has implications for political obligation. On the present interpretation, political obligation – the obligation to obey the law – is at least partly an obligation of juridical equals to contribute to the maintenance of the state, in proportion to their ability, under conditions of labour independence. Kant does not deny that the dependent producers have political obligations, but he does think that productive independence triggers special obligations.

---

[44] Davies argues that this passage makes citizenship track contribution to the state *in general*. This interpretation is too broad. Kant thinks that citizenship tracks contribution in the sense of citizenship being an attribute only of those who, as 'heads of households', possess an ability to produce a surplus which they realize by selling the surplus to other similarly situated surplus-producers. Crucially, these surplus-producers are dependent on the market *only for the sale of their surplus product*, not for their subsistence – their 'being fed and protected'. By contrast, those who lack a surplus-producing productive power, as well as those who produce a surplus for which there is no market, are not contributors to the commonwealth. They therefore do not contribute only *in that narrow sense*. This raises the question: what has surplus-production to do with the right to vote? Interdependent independence offers an answer to that question.

[45] See note 23, above.

Now, Kant's early characterization of citizenship in the loose sheets (see the *LDPP* passage above) is even more restrictive of the *demos* than the published account in *TP*. But it is in keeping with Kant's vision of the modern state as a system of interdependent independence, featuring cooperative production under a division of social labour. That vision brings the contradictory status of the dependent producer – at once formally free and equal but substantively dependent – into view. This contradiction will only become fully transparent in Marx's later discovery of the necessary unity between the egalitarianism of exchange and the inegalitarianism of production under capitalism.

I now explain why *Selbständigkeit*, read as interdependent independence, is exegetically superior to an alternative, property-based interpretation of Kantian citizenship.

2.6 The Mutual Irrelevance between Citizenship and Property

Interdependent independence takes Kant's concerns with property and propertylessness as wholly derivative from a more fundamental concern with the independent exercise of one's rightful powers as a member of the commonwealth. It therefore contrasts with a *proprietarian interpretation of civil self-sufficiency*.[46] According to that interpretation, you enjoy civil self-sufficiency if and only if your making a living depends exclusively on the exercise of your rightful property in external things. The proprietarian interpretation has numerous exegetical advantages. It explains why Kant takes domestic servants, minors, and women to lack self-sufficiency. It also explains Kant's insistence that property is a precondition of citizenship (*TP* 8: 295), as well as his belief that propertylessness – poverty – undermines self-sufficiency. This is ostensibly why he argues for state-provided poverty relief (*DR* 6: 326 f).[47] According to the proprietarian interpretation, the poor lack self-sufficiency because their making a living depends not *on their own property* but on the property rights and associated powers of the propertied, including their benevolence and goodwill.

Before proceeding, it might be worth explaining why the proprietarian interpretation is not tantamount to libertarianism and, more generally, why Kant is not a libertarian. Libertarianism is the idea that all rights flow from *ownership*, including self-ownership of one's body and its powers. In the *TP* passage elaborating on the conditions of citizenship, Kant writes that 'being one's own master (*sui juris*)' means 'having some *property* (and any craft, fine art, or science can be

---

[46] See Hruschka and Byrd (2012).
[47] Kant mentions state-provided poverty relief in passing in *DR* (6: 314) and defends it in *DR* (6: 326). For discussion of Kant's treatment of poverty, see Varden (2016) and E. Weinrib (2003). Note that the concept of economic dependence is logically weaker than that of poverty. I will return to this in Sections 2.6.1 and 3.3 below.

counted as property) ... that is, if he must acquire from others in order to live, he does so only by *alienating* what is *his*' (*TP* 8: 295). This would seem congenial to a comprehensive account of the possible objects of property, according to which the skilled are propertied, regardless of their ownership of external things. Indeed, if skill is property, then why not also the ability to work – one's *labour power*? This reflexive account of the possible objects of property entails libertarianism. Self-owners sell their property, including their own labour power, to other property owners, subject to a well-regulated system of contract and private property rights. Kant does not, however, affirm a reflexive account of property. He is therefore not a libertarian. Consider five reasons why Kant rejects libertarianism.

First, Kant explicitly denies that a person's body and its powers are ownable. These powers are the objects of *innate*, not acquired, right. And since all property rights are acquired rights (*DR* 6: 237), one's body and its powers are not ownable. Second, ownable objects have no rights (*DR* 6: 270), but persons do have rights, so persons are not ownable. Third, if mere skill and knowledge are property, then the skilled unemployed who lack rights to external things are not poor. But Kant does not exclude the skilled from poverty relief (*DR* 6: 326). Fourth, if possession of skill or mere labour power counts as property proper, then the skilled who lack external property – e.g. skilled domestic servants – cannot be counted as *passive* citizens. But Kant does so count them. Fifth, including skill or labour power as possible objects of property would make Kant's attempt to *justify* private property viciously circular. So property, for Kant, is not reflexive, as libertarians think. The proprietarian interpretation is narrower: it concerns property rights to *external things only*, not reflexive property rights to the owner and her powers.

Despite its numerous exegetical advantages, the proprietarian interpretation is inconsistent with Kant's texts. The inconsistency arises in empirical examples of two kinds: (i) examples involving *property but not civil self-sufficiency* and (ii) examples involving *self-sufficiency but not property*. In respect of (i), consider wage-labour. According to interdependent independence, wage-labour undermines self-sufficiency by making the exercise of the worker's productive powers dependent on the rights and powers of private employers – the owners of productive assets. This is true both for *finding* employment and for the *exercise* of these productive powers once in employment. Yet one can imagine a wage labourer whose income and wealth exceed those of Kant's civil servant and craftsman, both of whom are deemed to be juridically self-sufficient.[48] So in cases like the wage labourer, the proprietarian interpretation

---

[48] Moran (2021) makes a more general point about the merely formal nature of the wage labourer's dependence, which implies that such dependence does not presuppose poverty relative to other professions.

generates false positives.[49] In respect of (ii), consider cases of independent commodity production, in which each producer owns some, but not all, of the means of production she needs in order to set and pursue ends. Each can recover her purposiveness by selling to others the net product of the exercise of her unsubjected powers. In these kinds of cases, Kant allows for self-sufficiency without property in productive assets. So the proprietarian interpretation generates false negatives.

I now elaborate on these two kinds of cases, arguing for the exegetical superiority of interdependent independence over the proprietarian interpretation.

2.6.1 Property Is Insufficient for Selbständigkeit

I begin by defending two claims. First, *Selbständigkeit* as interdependent independence can account for all the empirical illustrations that the proprietarian interpretation can account for. Second, the proprietarian interpretation generates false positives, that is, deems as involving self-sufficiency cases that Kant deems as not involving self-sufficiency. If this is correct, then Kantian economic dependence is broader than poverty.

Consider first Kant's contrast between the Indian and the European blacksmith. This seems to support the proprietarian interpretation. After all, the Indian blacksmith lacks property in productive assets. But the proprietarian interpretation fails to account for Kant's contrast between private tutor and school teacher,[50] which says nothing about the private tutor's extent of property rights or her wealth and income. If the tutor's services are in especially high demand, for example, she might accumulate more property than the school teacher. By Kant's own lights, the tutor still lacks self-sufficiency. The proprietarian interpretation deems the rich private tutor self-sufficient. It therefore generates false positives.

Unlike the proprietarian interpretation, interdependent independence can account for the contrast. The tutor and Indian blacksmith, for example, lack self-sufficiency because they cannot make a living by exercising their productive powers (teaching, blacksmithing) without asking permission from the owner(s) of the conditions of production to exercise them. This dependence, Kant thinks,

---

[49] A false positive accepts the null hypothesis that 'this agent enjoys civil self-sufficiency' when the null hypothesis is, in fact, false. A false negative rejects the null hypothesis when it is, in fact, true.

[50] Hasan helpfully elaborates: 'in the case of the private tutor (passive citizen) versus the public school teacher (active citizen), the contrast seems to be that the tutor might have to tolerate abuses from a particular pupil or parents, because the fees they pay are necessary to sustain the tutor's survival, whereas the school teacher depends on a state salary and so can meaningfully reject behaviours that violate the terms of contract' (Hasan 2017, 922).

makes their productive agency *de facto* subordinate to the private choices of others and therefore makes *them* unfit to legislate rightfully.

2.6.2 Property Is Unnecessary for Selbständigkeit

I now argue for two further claims. First, the proprietarian interpretation generates false negatives, that is, deems as not involving civil self-sufficiency cases that Kant deems as involving self-sufficiency. Second, interdependent independence offers a systematic explanation for both sets of cases.

I begin with the first, anti-proprietarian, claim. Kant thinks that 'being fit to vote', serving 'no one other than the commonwealth', and 'being [your] own master' are extensionally equivalent. This is the Rousseauvian idea that, by giving coercive laws to yourself as free and equal, you are preserving your equal freedom *as such*.[51] Giving others permission to use your powers, by contrast, is a form of servitude. Kant elaborates:

> Someone who makes an *opus* can convey it to someone else by alienating it, just as if it were his property. But *praestatio operae* is not alienating something. A domestic servant, a shop clerk, a day laborer, or even a barber are merely *operarii*, not *artifices* (in the wider sense of the word) and not members of the state, and are thus also not qualified to be citizens. Although a man to whom I give my firewood to chop and a tailor to whom I give my cloth to make into clothes both seem to be in a quite similar relation to me, still the former differs from the latter, as a barber from a wigmaker (even if I have given him the hair for the wig) and hence as a day laborer from an artist or craftsman, who makes a work that belongs to him until he is paid for it. The latter, in pursuing his trade, thus exchanges his property with another (*opus*), the former, the use of his powers, which he grants to another (*operam*). (*TP* 8: 295)

The relevant contrast, for my purposes, is that between barber and wigmaker. The former, Kant says, is relevantly like domestic servants, shop clerks, and day labourers in that she must give others permission to use her powers. Not so in the case of the wigmaker, who can exercise her own powers independently of such use – she merely sells the *product* of that exercise. Crucially, Kant adds that the wigmaker enjoys civil self-sufficiency 'even if I have given him the hair for the wig'. The proprietarian interpretation, by contrast, deems the wigmaker to *lack* self-sufficiency, because she does not own hair. So the proprietarian interpretation generates false negatives. This argument impugns Rafeeq Hasan's proprietarian elaboration of the Indian blacksmith's status. Hasan suggests that, unlike the Indian blacksmith, the European blacksmith

---

[51] Relatedly, Kant emphasizes that taxation just means that 'the people taxes itself' (*DR* 6: 325).

owns not only his tools and his labor but also necessary raw materials. If he does not like the terms a particular customer offers and cannot find another buyer, he is still free to consume the product for himself, perhaps by decomposing it into its raw materials and selling those on the market, or trading his product for food. (Hasan 2017, 921)

The problem with this interpretation is that *both* wigmaker and Indian blacksmith lack raw materials (hair and iron, respectively). Yet, according to Kant, the former *is* her 'own master'. She is therefore self-sufficient.[52]

Interdependent independence can account for these contrasts. What matters for interdependent independence is not the origin of the subjection of the Indian blacksmith's labour. This could just be structurally conferred propertylessness, *à la* Hasan. Rather, what matters is only the fact that the blacksmith's setting and pursuing the end of iron production depends upon *giving others permission to use her productive powers to bring about that end*. As I understand him, Kant is saying that the concern with propertylessness is derivative of a more fundamental concern with unjustified control over the human productive powers, a proper subset of our powers as members of the commonwealth. Just like an orchestra of independent musicians, where each exercises her share of the musical powers unsubjected to alien private choices, so under legitimate public power each commonwealth member exercises her share of the productive powers unsubjected to alien private choices.[53] This makes her into an organic member of the commonwealth, acting 'in [productive – NV] community with others'. Each is simultaneously interdependent and independent.

So how is the hairless wigmaker self-sufficient and the ironless blacksmith not self-sufficient? By interdependent independence, you enjoy self-sufficiency if your (structurally-conferred) social position in the economy allows you to exercise your productive powers without having to give *other private persons* permission to use them. It is therefore possible that the wigmaker borrows hair from a merchant, which she uses to produce wigs, which she sells back to the merchant.[54] By contrast, if iron is very scarce or monopolized, then the blacksmith will not receive iron from a merchant in return for hammers. Instead, she

---

[52] Kant adds that only the wigmaker 'makes a work that belongs to him until he is paid for it' (*TP* 8:295). But this criterion cannot account for his other examples, such as the schoolteacher, who does not make anything that belongs to her until she is paid. Note that a civil servant barber is clearly self-sufficient, by Kant's own lights.

[53] Crucially, these powers are *unownable*, since Kant is not a libertarian (see Section 2.5).

[54] Wig merchants make money by selling wigs at the market price, so they must buy below that price. Note that Kant's own description of the origin of the wigmaker's inputs – 'I have given him the hair for the wig' – is unhelpful, because it poses the question anew: Where did I get the hair and how is the wigmaker guaranteed inputs after I run out? Kant himself would have been familiar with the *Verlagssystem*, the German version of the putting-out system, which began to flourish in Prussia in the middle of the eighteenth century (Kisch 1968).

will have to work *for* the iron owner(s).[55] This is how Kant can consistently hold that the wigmaker enjoys self-sufficiency, whereas the Indian blacksmith – who, by dint of inadequate access to capital, must alienate her powers – lacks it.[56]

If this hair-splitting interpretation of hair-splitting is correct, then one need not *own* all of one's production inputs to enjoy interdependent independence. Rather, the question seems to be whether, in general economic equilibrium, any agent or group *unilaterally controls the labour process of any other(s)*. Take a commodity economy of independent producers without a high concentration of labour-commanding pecuniary wealth. This was prevalent in Kant's time. In such conditions, even the hairless wigmaker can preserve her Kantian independence. The empirical form of interdependent independence is therefore independent commodity production.[57] Now contrast a capitalist economy, in which the concentration of labour-commanding wealth guarantees that some – the owners of that wealth – will unilaterally command alien labour.[58] According to Kant, this economy would make it impossible for the latter to legislate on behalf of their own agency. It would therefore deprive them of the formal standing to vote.

The empirical forms of interdependent independence are, of course, peripheral to Kant's political philosophy, which aims to justify externally coercive laws by appeal to an independent premiss about the conditions of citizenship. But the contrasts he draws between empirical cases ostensibly illustrating these conditions can only be coherently explained by appeal to interdependent independence: unsubjected formal discretion over one's rights and powers, including one's productive powers. Omnilateral rule, on this view, is constituted by free and equal citizens legislating on behalf of the stock of their rightful powers, which they can exercise independently of anyone's constraining private

---

[55] And if Prussian hair is as scarce as Indian iron – e.g. if too many Prussians are bald – then Kant's wigmaker may have to put her powers at the disposal of hair owners. Kantians may have overlooked the connection between freedom and baldness!

[56] It bears noting that access to capital need not involve *ownership* of capital, which could be borrowed.

[57] Williams (2006, 376) argues that Kant is here envisaging the independence of a nascent 'middle class'. The term is ambiguous across a feudal 'middle class', which effectively designates nascent capitalists, and a capitalist 'middle class', which effectively designates the petty bourgeoisie. On my interpretation, Kant is defending the latter.

[58] In the section on 'What Is Money?', immediately following his discussion of contract, Kant argues that money is 'the universal means by which men exchange their industriousness [*Fleiss*] with one another' (*DR* 6:287). The next paragraph offers an inchoate statement of Adam Smith's labour theory of value. Many have noted that Kant has a limited conception of civil society, such that Smithian 'commercial society' and the role of capital only feature incidentally in his writings. But Kant sees further than his contemporaries, in trying to enfranchise productive purposiveness – labour power – and the division of labour into his theory of the state.

choices.[59] Interdependent independence, I submit, is the only consistent treatment of Kant's discussion of the ideal and empirical forms of citizenship.

To sum up the argument of this section: Kant thinks that public power enjoys legitimacy only insofar as it legislates on behalf of free, equal, and independent citizens. It follows that a public power legislating on behalf of economically dependent citizens would lack legitimacy. This is why Kant – eager to preserve the legitimacy of public power but under no illusions about the pervasiveness of dependence – is wont to disenfranchise the dependent. But Kant's obsolete distinction between active and passive citizens has a singular virtue. Unlike contemporary Kantian defences of the liberal capitalist state, fidelity to Kant's own position need not pretend that the denizens of such a state can all be independent. For all its emphasis on inclusion, liberal capitalism presupposes that some of its co-legislators must remain dependent on the unilateral will of some ruling class. The revolutionary implication is to preserve the spirit of Kant's argument by guaranteeing all members of the commonwealth independent use of their interdependent rightful powers.

I now explain how this thought takes us beyond an influential liberal interpretation of Kant's political philosophy.

3 Kantian Independence beyond Liberalism

Section 2 argued that Kant thinks of citizenship in terms of interdependent independence: the independent use of citizens' interdependent rightful powers. This section explains how interdependent independence takes us beyond an influential liberal interpretation of Kantian citizenship. According to this 'Toronto' interpretation, the Kantian objection to economic dependence is fundamentally about poverty. Eliminate poverty – read: propertylessness – and you have eliminated economic dependence. So Kant's political economy of citizenship *just is* the dialectic of property and propertylessness under the modern state. This section argues that interdependent independence extends beyond propertylessness. Economic independence, for Kant, is co-extensive with self-standing (*selbstständig*) production for a competitive market – independent commodity production. It follows that Kant's political economy of citizenship is not fundamentally about property and propertylessness, but rather about the independent exercise of the productive capacities of free and equal people.

This section is structured as follows. I begin by elaborating on the Toronto interpretation. I then focus on its implications for redistribution and the welfare

---

[59] Nonworkers, including the disabled, can share in this representation insofar as they are supported by the state: as its *members*, they have a stake in and share of control over the commonwealth's powers, including its productive powers.

state. After reviewing relevant passages from Kant on economic independence, I show that these passages do not support the narrow Toronto focus on property. I then argue that they support a broader, productive agency reading. I conclude by highlighting some contrasts on the topic of economic dependence between Kant, Hegel, and Marx, on the one hand, and Kant and Rawls, on the other.

3.1 The Antilibertarian Gambit

Suppose that the British government decides to privatize the roads and sidewalks. And suppose that the putative justification for this policy is not efficiency, but ostensibly equal freedom. Perhaps the British government consists of tough-minded luck egalitarians, who think that everyone should own an equal share of road and sidewalk. What could one object to this policy, on grounds of equal freedom? A devastating objection is that it would make every commuter subject to the private choices of each individual road owner. That is, even if every citizen owned an equal road share, such ownership would make the purposiveness of all subject to the purposes of each. I am not free to move around if my movement depends on your permission, even if you're inclined to grant it. So this government policy would violate every commuter's right to equal freedom.

This kind of objection is central to the debate between G.A. Cohen (1995) and Robert Nozick (1974) on the nature of property rights. One of Cohen's dialectical arguments against Nozick's use of the term 'liberty' in *Anarchy, State, and Utopia* asks whether Lockean self-ownership[60] protects individual autonomy. To show that it does not, Cohen imagines a system of joint ownership, in which everyone must get permission from others to perform any external action, including the occupation of physical space. Cohen then asks whether such a system would be compatible with the form of self-ownership prized by Nozickian libertarians. Suppose, on the one hand, that self-ownership and joint ownership *are* compatible. Then self-ownership is no freedom at all, for it is consistent with having to ask permission from others to set and pursue any possible end.[61] Suppose, on the other hand, that self-ownership and joint ownership are *not* compatible. Then capitalist private property draws exactly the same objection as joint ownership – the value of being able to independently pursue ends requires a state more extensive than a minimal state. That is, effective self-ownership requires a state providing poverty relief and redistributing wealth so that nobody requires permission from others to pursue her ends.[62]

---

[60] On Kant on self-ownership, see Section 2.6.
[61] This argument is highly reminiscent of Kant's discussion of the original communism of property. See Section 2.1.
[62] I discuss and defend Cohen's argument in Vrousalis (2015).

This argument has a distinctly antilibertarian flavour, because it starts from a premiss about the external *freedom* of the poor, not about their needs or welfare. It has been revived in the work of Ernest Weinrib (2003) and Arthur Ripstein (2009) – the 'Toronto Kantians'. One of their contributions to the debate has been to add more flesh to Cohen's barebones argument against libertarianism, taking their cue from Kant's political philosophy. I begin by elaborating on this social-democratic – 'liberal' – strand in Kant exegesis.

3.2 Taking Toronto Roads Seriously

The Toronto Kantians, especially Ripstein, think there is something special about roads. The term 'roads' doubles up in meaning here: it signifies roads, but also any all-purpose means (e.g. law, knowledge, health, education). So here is Ripstein, discussing the problem of the landlocked commuter:

> Private ownership of land does not simply foreclose some particular purpose that you might happen to have, but also forecloses the entire formal class of purposes involving voluntary interaction with others. The problem is formal, because it does not depend on the particular purposes for which any two persons might wish to interact, but rather on the fact that they are subject to a third person from whom they must secure permission to interact. (Ripstein 2009, 247)

As his fellow Toronto Kantian Chris Essert puts it, lacking a road is unlike lacking a boat; roadlessness is unlike boatlessness in that having a boat serves a narrow set of ends (Essert 2017). Roadlessness, by contrast, deprives you of access to *any* end involving proximity to others; it deprives you of end-setting capacity *tout court*. 'The solution to this problem is obvious: roads, understood as a system of public rights of way, guaranteeing that there is a path from every piece of privately held land to every other' (Ripstein 2009, 248). The contrast between boatlessness and roadlessness can be extended further. Consider homelessness. Homelessness is not just lack of a home, because a homeless person can consistently have access to shelter. So her problem is not lack of housing but lack of an enforceable *right* to a home (Essert 2017). In lacking such a right, she is subject to the permission of *some* landowner or other, even if they are (individually or collectively) inclined to grant it. So homelessness draws the same objection as roadlessness.

Now, one of the core ambitions of Toronto Kantianism is to show that private property requires, for its justification, a system of omnilateral rights guaranteeing each her independence. Ripstein argues that this presupposes economic redistribution:

> This argument for economic redistribution is *internal* to the idea that acquisition must be authorized and disputes resolved through public procedures that can be accepted by all. Absent institutions of public justice, the rich person's claim to exclude the poor from her property would just be a unilateral imposition of force. Those who have property have the right to exclude provided that their holdings of property are consistent with a united will shared by all – that the system of private rights really is part of a system of equal independence of free persons. (Ripstein 2009, 283)

It follows that the Kantian state must provide *publicly funded* poverty relief. Recall that Kant's argument for the liberal state starts from a premiss about independence: you cannot give yourself laws that would make you into the servant of another. The Toronto interpretation adds that a system of laws which countenances poverty – propertylessness – would turn the poor into servants of property. So poverty is not in conformity with right. More succinctly: free and equal people cannot covenant their way into poverty. To do so would be to 'throw away their freedom' (*DR* 6: 329). It follows that the Kantian state must include *mandatory* coercive redistribution from the propertied to the propertyless. Kant explicitly supports this conclusion when he writes that

> Having the resources to practice such beneficence as depends on the goods of fortune is, for the most part, a result of certain human beings being favoured through the *injustice of government*, which introduces an inequality of wealth that makes others need their beneficence. (MM 6: 454, emphasis added)

On this reading, Kant was a social democrat before it was cool.

Now note that the Toronto position is stronger than Cohen's, because it asserts the necessity of redistribution *coerced by public laws*. It would not, in other words, suffice if some philanthrocapitalists got together and offered poor relief equal to what a Kantian state would offer. Oprah-funded poverty relief is necessarily unjust when Leviathan-funding is available. Cohen's joint-ownership scenario, by contrast, allows private persons to accommodate the external actions of others. Again, the problem with this move is that Oprah's permission is always revocable *by Oprah's private will*.[63] This is why the Toronto argument is more robustly egalitarian than Cohen's.

I now explain how Kant's treatment of work shows his views of economic independence to be even more demanding than Toronto liberalism allows. To

---

[63] What if Oprah has no such discretion, but retains beneficial ownership? Suppose that, by state mandate, she does not legislate the permissions for receiving poor relief but retains rights to the residual (the state pays her rent from general taxation or gives her tax cuts). This seems equivalent to the state coercing me to pay you not to kill me. The correct policy is to hinder your attempt to kill – not to get me to pay you not to do it. The Toronto view, by contrast, seems consistent with these powers remaining Oprah's, even if she is constrained to exercise them for public purposes.

anticipate the rest of the argument, suppose that public roads are of low quality compared to private roads, to such an extent that everyone prefers private to public roads. Then, *pace* Ripstein, Toronto's public roads do not solve the problem of mutual dependence. What we need, instead, is a set of public roads that minimize or altogether eliminate the extent of private discretion over our *walking* lives. By the same token, a system of public right that only gives us some property but allows full private discretion over our *working* lives would be similarly unjustified. So Toronto leaves us unfree in both our walking and our working lives. I now make the case for this conclusion.

3.3 Kant beyond Toronto

In Section 2, I argued that if the blacksmith in India lacks iron ownership, then she lacks independent use of her productive powers. In order to exercise these powers, she must get permission from the iron owner(s) to use the iron they own. This means she must put her powers at their disposal. And this is why Kant disenfranchises her, on the grounds of lacking civil self-sufficiency. None of these inferences makes sense unless Kant thinks of the rightful condition as a system of cooperative production, in which the subjection of labour capacity to a private will undermines one's formal standing to legislate universally.

Now, Kant's discussion of the two blacksmiths asserts a *discriminating position*: the European blacksmith is independent, whereas the Indian blacksmith is not. What explains this asymmetry? The Toronto answer is that only the latter is poor. But one can imagine the Indian blacksmith possessing property equal to that of Kant's civil servant, craftsman, and European blacksmith. Yet only the latter are dubbed independent.[64] So Kantian economic dependence must be broader than propertylessness. More precisely: *propertylessness is sufficient but unnecessary for unjust economic dependence*. How, then, does Kant propose to spell out the necessary condition? The answer, I think, must have something to do with the independent possession and use of one's powers. To insulate the rest of my exegesis from Toronto liberalism, I will hereafter assume that wage labourers are not poorer than the median public servant – perhaps because there is high demand for labour, or there is public poverty relief, or an unconditional basic income. Being empirical, these assumptions do not beg the question against Toronto. I now explain how economic dependence, for Kant, extends beyond poverty.

A central step towards understanding Kant's affirmation of the discriminating position must look to the role he assigns to the market. On the present

---

[64] Moran (2021) makes a more general point about the merely formal nature of the wage labourer's dependence, which implies that such dependence does not presuppose poverty.

interpretation, the European blacksmith produces for a competitive market in a self-standing way, that is, not for a boss or a series thereof (*DR* 6: 315). This is what I called *independent commodity production*. Independent commodity production, for Kant, guarantees the productive independence of interdependent people. But now notice that we are already outside Toronto territory, since independent commodity production requires more than property ownership. After all, the Indian and European blacksmith might own the same amount of property. Yet Kant only dubs the latter as 'self-standing'.

An obvious rejoinder is that there is no discrimination to be had here. If nobody wants to buy the European blacksmith's *hammers*, then she will starve. By the same token, if nobody wants to hire the Indian blacksmith's *labour*, then he will starve. Therefore there is no sustainable discriminating position between the two cases – dependence on a series of consumers through the product market and dependence on a series of bosses through the labour market. Kant's response to this objection is remarkably consistent across *TP* and *DR*. It consists in his distinction between *opus* and *operam*[65] – that is, between

(1) private discretion over the use of your powers

vs.

(2) private discretion over the *product* of the use of your powers

The distinction between (1) and (2) is basically a distinction between markets for labour, on the one hand, and markets for goods and services, on the other.[66] Kant's implicit assumption must be that competitive markets for goods and services draw a justification that labour (and capital) markets do not. For only the former are indispensable to the coordination of production and consumption. In Waheed Hussain's (2023) apt expression, competitive markets for goods and services constitute a public 'pattern of practical reasoning' that coordinates the behaviour of private actors in a way that would otherwise be impossible to achieve. Capital and labour markets, on the other hand, are unnecessary for that allocative role, so they do not draw the same justification. Moreover, as I explained above, (2) alone is in conformity with independence, because (2) alone is consistent with the producer legislating on behalf of her own productive agency, independently of the productive choices of others. If that argument is sound, then Kant has a case for discriminating between his two sets of examples.

---

[65] See *TP* 8:295 and *DR* 6:314. The first passage, cited in Section 2.6.2 above, contrasts *opus* (singular nominative) with *operam* (singular accusative). The difference in declension highlights the fact that dependent labour involves alienation of one's *powers*, in addition to the product of their exercise.

[66] To buy a service is not to buy the *labour capacity* of the service provider. Kant presciently recognizes this distinction in *DR* 6:361.

Of course, Kant accepts that independent commodity production implies market dependence. The European blacksmith depends on the will of the consumers as a whole. But this is just shorthand for dependence on the material preconditions of the just state. It is therefore dependence on the conditions for the freedom of all: 'Thus a nation's wealth, insofar as it is acquired by means of money, is really only *the sum of the industry with which human beings pay one another* and which is represented in the money in circulation within it' (*DR* 6: 287, emphasis added).[67] Such dependence on the mere 'sum of industry' contrasts with the Indian blacksmith's dependence on the private will of a (series of) private employers. So the European blacksmith, but not the Indian blacksmith, can self-legislate, in the sense that s*he can make arrangements for herself with what is hers*. The exercise of her powers is not permissionally conditional on someone else's – only the sale of her product is.[68] No other reading makes sense of Kant's consistent assertion of the discriminating position and its associated contrasts.

This kind of argument would be roundly criticized by Marx some sixty years later. In the *Grundrisse*, Marx argues that independent commodity production – independent, small-scale production for a competitive market – is compatible with a set of merchants, usurers, or protocapitalists coming to control the net product. This means that they possess an ownership-conferred power over the labour capacities of others, *even if they are not anyone's boss* and *even if markets are perfectly competitive*.[69] This is possible because some market actors (in competition with each other) can command more labour than they give in its production. This possibility, broached by Smith in *The Wealth of Nations*, was hardly applicable to the port economy of eighteenth-century Königsberg, Kant's city.

But the road to Manchester may yet *begin* in Königsberg. Kant's insistence on independent commodity production, although unrealizable under mechanized industry, suggests that he is not just interested in poverty as propertylessness, as the Toronto interpretation suggests. I now present another example that builds on

---

[67] Note that Kant's focus on money in exchange for *industry* equivocates between money as money and money as *capital*, that is, as monetized control over alien labour capacity. I discuss the difference in Vrousalis (2023, chapter 2).

[68] Kant's discussion of the labour contract is one of the origins of Marx's account of the 'fetishism of the commodity' in *Capital* (Marx 1976, 163f). This is the idea that, under capitalism alone, the hierarchical relation between capital and labour in the sphere of production (a 'relation between persons') *necessarily* appears as a relationship between owners of commodities in the sphere of exchange (a 'relation between things'). Crucially, Marx will argue that the labour contract is *both* of these things. This exactly mirrors Kant's treatment of judgement and intuition in the first *Critique*.

[69] '[T]he merchant induces a number of weavers and spinners, who until then wove and spun as a rural, secondary occupation, to work for him, making their secondary into their chief occupation; but then he has them in his power and has brought them under his command as wage labourers' (Marx 1973, 510ff.).

the distinction between (1) and (2). Suppose that omelettes are the only means of consumption and that, if I am to nourish myself, I must produce an omelette. As long as you and others own the eggs, I can produce the omelette only by your permission, which makes my ability to set and pursue the end of omelette production – my productive purposiveness – subordinate to your unilateral will. Omelette redistribution will not solve this problem, insofar as it leaves the mode of omelette *production* untouched, no matter how much it ameliorates the mode of omelette *distribution* in my favour. Egalitarian egg *pre*distribution does better, but still subordinates my omelette production to your will, insofar as it does not preclude your ownership and control over the omelette-producing cookshop. Independent commodity production, Kant thinks, features *neither* form of subjection: in producing for the market with their own inputs, independent commodity producers are subject neither to the power of the lords nor to the power of the rich.[70] Whether or not Kant is right to think this, it follows that Kant's political economy of citizenship is not fundamentally about property and propertylessness. It is, rather, about forms of power over the productive capacities of the direct producers.

To sum up the argument so far: Kant says that those who cannot make arrangements about themselves, including the poor, cannot legislate on behalf of their own agency. They are therefore unfit to vote (*DR* 6: 315). But later in the same text he broaches the possibility that they need not be disenfranchised if given enough property to legislate on behalf of their own agency (*DR* 6: 326). I have argued that Kant's examples evince the same ambivalence about wage labour: should it be abolished or should its agents be disenfranchised? The ambivalence arises because if nobody can covenant into property as her master, then nobody can covenant into *capitalist* property as her master. But then eliminating poverty (as general propertylessness) is only a subset of economic independence. The Toronto interpretation's emphasis on propertylessness cannot account for this conclusion. Interdependent independence can.

I now explain what this interpretation has to say about a related but neglected issue: the gendered and racialized division of labour.

3.4 Race and Gender

According to Kant, Private Right is subdivided into three categories: property, contract, and status.[71] The third category involves 'a right to a person akin to a right to a thing', which makes certain uses of other humans 'provisionally rightful' (e.g. of a child until majority or of a marriage partner) in ways that

---

[70] I discuss variants of this example in Vrousalis (2023).
[71] See Brosch (2024) for a recent overview.

would be impossible without law (*DR* 6: 276). More specifically, the subsumption of external things (property), of the 'causality' of others (contract), and of domestic society (status) under relations of Private Right makes labour flows *within* these relations provisionally rightful. Now suppose, through no great stretch of the imagination, that care work is overwhelmingly performed by women and migrants. It follows that Kantian Private Right establishes provisionally rightful labour flows that are gendered and racialized. Jordan Pascoe (2022) has recently argued, on this basis, that Kantian citizenship entails a set of unjust claims, on the part of a *white male ruling class*, to the surplus labour of gendered and racialized humans. More precisely, Pascoe argues that the domestic labour of migrants and women under Kantian Right is structurally dependent – as is standard wage-labour – but is *also* gendered and racialized – unlike standard wage-labour.

For the sake of concreteness, consider the following schematic representation of labour flows under Private Right. There are three hierarchically related groups: the *A*s are active citizens, engaged in 'self-standing' market transactions with each other. The *B*s are passive citizens engaged in wage-labour for the *A*s. The *C*s are also passive citizens, but this time in 'status' relationships with the *A*s and *B*s as 'heads of households' (*DR* 6: 282). In Kant's characterization of domestic society, the Category includes wives, domestic servants, and children. There are two forms of interdependence here: horizontal (between the *A*s) and vertical (between the *A*s, on the one hand, and the *B*s and *C*s, on the other). Crucially, in all vertical relationships labour flows unilaterally from the subordinates (the *B*s and *C*s) to the superordinates (the *A*s). With this schema in mind, I now return to Pascoe's treatment of Kant.

I agree with Pascoe that Kant's account of citizenship implies *de facto* claims, by a white male ruling class, to the alien labour capacities of other humans. This much follows from interdependent independence.[72] But there are some contrasts between Pascoe's account and mine. First, Pascoe claims that the reigning injustice here is 'coerced cooperation' (Pascoe 2022, 50). This is misleading. For Kant, coercion is a feature of every just society and a necessary complement to independent cooperation. This is why, for example, an able-bodied rich person can be rightfully coerced to contribute to general taxation in the interest of the freedom of a disabled poor person. Such coercion, according to Kant, would only be tantamount to a 'hindering of a hindrance to freedom' (*DR* 6:231). This is significant, because some coercible entitlements to one's product are not generically objectionable from the point of view of rightful freedom.

---

[72] Interdependent independence has the further implication that class, gender, and racial oppression are fundamentally about control over *labour capacity* (see Fraser 2023; Vrousalis 2023).

The *A*s, for example, may have coercible entitlements to each other's labour contribution or its fruits, consistently with everyone's independence.

But perhaps Pascoe is objecting to power over the total *stock* of labour capacities, not the *flow* that constitutes their exercise. That is, the problem seems to be that the *B*s and *C*s are subordinate to the *A*s, because the latter *dominate* the former. This domination means that the *A*s, as a whole, are entitled not to alien labour but rather to the use of the stock of labour *capacities* of the *B*s and *C*s. The exercise of those capacities constitutes unjust labour flow.[73] And if Pascoe is right about the 'enclosed dependence' of migrants and women under domestic right, then the *C*s are excluded from the benefits of social cooperation. They are, therefore, in addition to being exploited, extorted. This is consistent with my interpretation of Kant.

Another contrast between Pascoe's interpretation and mine pertains to Pascoe's reading of Public Right, which implies that interdependence precludes Kantian independence. But surely the latter presupposes the former. More precisely, the *A*s are active citizens, who are reciprocally *horizontally* interdependent and also *vertically* interdependent with the *B*s and *C*s. Kant does see the problem with vertical interdependence – dependent labour – but dismisses it by allowing that any of those below can 'work his way up from [passive citizenship] to an active one' (*DR* 6:316). Pascoe is right to highlight the consistency of upward mobility with structural unfreedom. She does not, however, provide an explanation of *how* the disenfranchisement of the *B*s and *C*s is supposed to be justified, on Kant's account. Interdependent independence fills this gap.

Crucially, according to interdependent independence, Kant's disenfranchisement of passive citizens is *only* about dependent labour. So it can have nothing to do, in the first instance, the ascription of gender and race.[74] A good example is Kant's judgement of Kant himself. In *DR* 6:315 Kant contrasts the private tutor with the schoolteacher, claiming that only the latter performs independent (*selbständig*) labour. So only the latter is an active citizen – a citizen with a right to vote. Yet, as Pascoe points out, no relevant *empirical* feature of Kant's changes in his transition from being a private tutor (in the 1740's) to a university professor (in the 1770's). This claim is generalizable. That is, no cognitive or motivational feature, or its ascription to some putative race or gender, plays any

---

[73] This is why Kant is so keen to distinguish between persons and their powers, where the latter can be contracted out only for limited purposes and for a limited time (see, for example, *DR* 6:285 and *TP* 8:295). I elaborate on the distinction further in Vrousalis (2023), where I also explain why Marx was justified in criticizing its application to the labour contract.

[74] 'In the first instance': assuming that there is no past injustice or that all past injustice has been rectified. See Weinrib (1995) for a seminal treatment of Kant's theory of corrective justice.

role in Kant's account of independent labour. This is the only condition necessary and sufficient for the transition from passive to active citizenship. As I explained in Section 2.5, this contradicts a mainstream neo-Roman reading of independence.

This brings me to a final point. Most of Kant's political writings are produced in the 1790s. They contain scarcely any association of Right with the putative cognitive and motivational dispositions of racialized and gendered humans. Kant does think of unilaterally determined purposiveness as merely sensuous and so not as an intellectual part of the republic. But this is not because dependent labour – and *therefore* racialized or gendered labour – cannot subsume sensibility to intellect. Rather, it is because that determinative power, when rightfully exercised, is de facto subject to the alien will of some ruling class. By definition, ruling classes rule through control over labour, whether or not that labour is gendered or racialized. So Kant's disenfranchising exclusions, although unjustifiable, evince a fundamental concern about the independent determination of one's sensuous powers, including her labour power, to the constitution of public power.

There is an interesting parallel here between Kant and Toussaint L'Ouverture, the Haitian revolutionary and founder of modern Haiti. Pascoe discusses a famous passage, in which Kant argues that a slavery contract is impossible. Kant mentions Haiti by name ('the Sugar Islands') and broaches an alternative to wage-labour: the possibility of 'someone' – presumably an emancipated slave – contracting to work 'on his master's land in exchange *for the use of it* instead of receiving wages' (*DR* 6:330, my emphasis).

It is not far-fetched to suppose that Kant was here applying his third category of Private Right to the institutions of a possible post-slavery Haiti. L'Ouverture, for his part, had to invent a much more authoritarian version of the same category. In the 1801 constitution of Haiti he instituted a system of forced, plantation-based sharecropping, in which the contractual obligations of planters were to be overseen and enforced by the governor (see Hazareesingh 2020, 401 n.88). So L'Ouverture was forced to institute, in practice, the same juridical category of right, lying between slavery and wage-labour, that Kant had invented in theory. In both cases, the putative justification for that category seems to have arisen neither from paternalistic opposition to idleness nor from any racialized assumptions about the dispositions of 'lazy freedmen', as Pascoe interprets Kant (Pascoe 2022, 39 f). Rather, it arose from a commitment to mandatory cooperation as the material basis for the freedom and equality of all, under scarcely propitious circumstances. I now explain how these ideas extend to one specific form of racialized labour, namely migrant labour.

Kant's account of Public Right comprises, in addition to rightful intrastate relations, rightful interstate relations (the 'Right of Nations'), as well as rightful relations between states and individuals or non-state entities ('Cosmopolitan Right'). Sylvie Loriaux has argued that rich states, according to Kant, may have redistributive duties to poor states. The ground of these duties is securing the 'preconditions of self-determination' for poor states as part of a global civil condition (Loriaux 2020, 47). These duties are not coercible, but only subject to interstate agreement. Since this Element is about intrastate relations, I will not discuss interstate and cosmopolitan right.[75] Yet there is, Loriaux argues, another class of duties to migrants from poor to rich states that are strictly *intra*state:

> If the 'increasing scarcity of inhabitable land' cannot be detached from a global network of complex relationships in which all inhabitants of the planet are in one way or another implicated, the admission of migrants on foreign territory may also present itself as a duty of rectificatory justice. (Loriaux 2020, 55)

On this view, European states have duties of justice to, say, Indian migrants, insofar as the former are implicated in the plight of the latter. Kant mentions colonialism, war, and fraudulent trade practices as forms of that plight. Loriaux is surely right that these are Kantian grounds for an open migration policy. But interdependent independence seems more demanding than Loriaux allows. For there is little by way of justification that Kant's Europeans can offer to Indian migrants for denying them not just admission but *citizenship*. That is, Kant's disenfranchising exclusions clearly apply to all dependent labour, whether performed by indigenous or by migrant workers. To return to Kant's own example, the European blacksmith owns means of production. She therefore enjoys civil self-sufficiency and so is enfranchised. The Indian blacksmith, by contrast, owns no means of production. She therefore does not enjoy civil self-sufficiency and so is not enfranchised. Interdependent independence turns this QED into a *reductio*. Even if it were admitted that the rights and obligations of citizenship extend only to intrastate relations, they must cover not just the indigenous population but also in-state immigrants, such as blacksmiths from India.[76] At least this much seems to follow from Kant's own ambivalent

---

[75] But see Williams (2006), who argues that independence provides a bottom-up account of cosmopolitan solidarity across citizens of different states. This feature provides an impetus for the international confederation of republics geared towards 'a universal and perpetual peace'. This, Kant thinks, is 'the entire final end of the doctrine of right' (DR 6: 355). On the connection between cosmopolitanism and property, see Pinheiro Walla (2020) and Huber (2022).

[76] A more radical move would turn this into an argument for global citizenship. That is, given the extent of interstate interdependence under globalized production, there is little by way of justification for the privileges of citizenship. So if Kant's rich blacksmith can offer very little to a poor blacksmith in justification for her socioeconomic privilege in Europe, then there will be

assertion of the priority of independence over property. This concludes my discussion of racialized labour.

I now explain how variants of the idea of interdependent independence point the way towards a more radical critique of socioeconomic inequality, through Hegel and Marx, up to Rawls.

3.5 From Kant to Rawls, through Hegel and Marx

Interdependent independence establishes a presumption against power over the productive capacities of others. It is a 'presumption' because there are all kinds of special justifications for such power.[77] One such justification is the existence of public offices. To produce under the direct authority of a public office, assuming it is geared towards the freedom and equality of all, is to serve the conditions of everyone's freedom, including one's own. It is therefore to serve only the conditions of one's rightful freedom – to 'make arrangements about yourself' as free and equal. Kant's contrasts between domestic and civil servant, private tutor and school teacher, copyholder and freeholder, all seem to presuppose this exculpating condition on power. How else could the same labour *content* (delivering letters, teaching students, cultivating the land) have different freedom valence across Kant's contrasts?

But, as I explained in Section 3.3, Kant's *DR* contrast between the two blacksmiths and his *TP* contrast between barber and wigmaker suggests a different special justification for power over productive capacity. That justification is self-standing production for a competitive market. This is a market in which producers are not necessarily poor or subject to the unilateral authority of bosses. Consumers in this market have power over producers, but that is unlike the power employers have over employees. Crucially, this is the only way to make sense of Kant's consistent assertion of the discriminating position in all of his writings on work. Marx's later criticism of the discriminating position, and his concomitant distinction between labour and labour power, shows that Kant's argument can only be sustained under very restrictive conditions, namely under conditions where the capitalist mode of production does not predominate. But both Kant and Marx may be right: the former was wrong only about the restricted applicability of an otherwise sound principle. So the reason Toronto

---

very little she can offer to a poor blacksmith *in India*. See Julius (2003) and Ypi (2014) for different arguments that the demands of global justice are increasing in global interdependence.

[77] The existence of public power as a system of omnilateral authorization has certain necessary presuppositions for public power to be *thinkable* as such. These powers must include legal powers of public officials over other public officials, legal powers of voters over public officials, a separation of jurisdictional powers across different branches of government (*DR* 6: 313), and so on. See Ripstein (2009).

liberalism is inadequate is that Kant takes production, social reproduction, and their material conditions as *themselves* subject to the innate right to freedom. In a nutshell, Toronto neglects the supply-side of Right.

A corollary of Kant's treatment of the market is a 'dialectic' of labour, or something resembling a materialist theory of history.[78] Although Kant does not say so explicitly, *DR* adverts to the form of *interdependent* independence that comes with independent commodity production. That is, Kant's conception of the independent free and equal citizen starts from the assumption of equal legal subjects. He proceeds by adding qualifications, including their market relationships, that justify ascribing *citizenship* status to them. Marx's mode of operation in *Capital* is similar. He begins from the equal legal status of reciprocally-situated commodity owners. He proceeds by adding qualifications that would justify ascribing *capitalist* status to them. In both cases, the ascription (being a citizen, being a capitalist) is existentially dependent on, and derived from, *the form of labour extracted or performed*. In this sense, the road to Manchester must necessarily begin in Königsberg.

This 'dialectic of labour' is substantiated in Kant's discussion of the foundations of the state in the *Conjectural Beginning of Human History*. Here Kant surmises that 'the human being passed over from the period of comfort and peace into that of *labour* and *discord*, as the prelude to the unification in society' (*CB* 8: 118, emphases in original). Since the division of labour and the concomitant 'discord' are indispensable to progress, the only way to humanize them is through the *institutionalization* of independence. Echoing Rousseau, Kant adds that this requires an 'external lawfulness, … civil right', which obtains because 'the human being was to *labour himself* out of the crudity of his natural predispositions by himself, and yet was to take care not to offend against them even as he elevates himself above them' (CB 8: 117, emphasis mine). My interpretation explains how this enfranchisement of specifically human production might work as part of Kant's broader theory of justice.

Now, Kant could not have been a socialist, any more than Plato could have been a Christian. Like his contemporary Sieyès, Kant's main concern was to eradicate the juridical vestiges of feudalism. But Kant went further than Sieyès, by thinking of the modern state as a system of cooperative production, in which our reciprocal entitlements to one another's labour carry a justificatory burden. Moreover, the application of the idea of *Selbständigkeit* to the modern capitalist

---

[78] On Kant's philosophy of history, see Wood (2005). Marx's 'dialectic' of labour in the *Grundrisse* starts from the primitive independence of the individual under precapitalist societies. This distinguishes it from the subsumed interdependence of the individual under capitalism. The antinomy is resolved under the free individuality of communist society. See Marx (1973, 495f).

state unearths a tension between citizenship and poverty. Its full import culminates in Marx's *Critique of Political Economy*, half a century after Kant:

> Kant would acknowledge that the empirical conditions within the State prevent the freedom envisaged by the idea of the State from being realized. The formal equality of each person within civil society is empirically contradicted by his actual economic and social dependence on other persons. (Williams 1983, 180–181)

According to interdependent independence, this 'contradiction' follows from Kant's understanding of the proper object of universal legislation in the modern state. Most theories of citizenship since Kant have had to grapple, implicitly or explicitly, with this problem.

It may be useful to contrast Kant and Hegel here. In the *Philosophy of Right*, Hegel redoubles on Kant's praise for commerce and the division of labour, which he calls 'the system of needs'. Hegel goes as far as to argue that 'civil society' – the market system – is the distinguishing feature of modernity. He claims that the development of modern civil society expresses a 'subjective particularity . . . allowed its rights'. This 'becomes the animating principle of the entire civil society, of the development alike of mental activity, merit, and dignity' (Hegel 2015, 133). For Hegel, labour under the liberal institutions of modernity completes the human being as such. So Hegel, like Kant, thinks of the 'self-standing' citizen as the pinnacle of modernity.

But Hegel also highlights the dangers of economic instability and poverty inherent in the market system. And although he does not yet recognize the possibility of a specifically capitalist mode of production, he does identify poverty as a recurring, inescapable, and destructive feature of civil society. Poverty is inescapable, Hegel thinks, because it results from the mechanization of production and the concomitant – he thinks – drop in wages and employment. It is destructive because it tends to dissolve the estates[79] into opposing classes. This threatens the very existence of the modern state. So, although Kant and Hegel offer different solutions to the problem of poverty,[80] both disenfranchise the poor for similar reasons: Kant, because the poor cannot freely self-legislate; Hegel, because they jeopardize the stability of free institutions. Crucially, both Kant and Hegel take the connection between labour and poverty to be central to the constitution of modern citizenship. The connection remains central to contemporary political philosophy.

---

[79] In Hegel's theory of the state, the estates comprise agriculture, commerce and manufacturing, and a post-Napoleonic bureaucracy (the 'universal class').

[80] Hegel does not regard public poverty relief as a solution to the problem of poverty, but rejects all other extant solutions. See Hardimon (2009) and McNulty (2023).

I conclude this section by contrasting the Kantian picture of cooperative production with Rawls'. Rawls (2001) famously criticizes welfare-state capitalism for being too lenient on inequality and therefore on the economic conditions of equal citizenship. Rawls' view is, in that respect, more demanding than Toronto liberalism. It is therefore more in line with Kant's, as I have presented him. In his later writings, Rawls explicitly endorses 'property-owning democracy' (egalitarian predistribution) and 'liberal socialism' (state-owned means of production plus worker cooperatives) as the only two eligible institutional arrangements for 'justice as fairness'. This is how Rawls proposes to enfranchise 'powers and prerogatives of offices and authority' into the subject of justice. Now suppose that these powers fall under the purview of his 'difference principle',[81] and that work involves such powers. There is, then, no reason why a Rawlsian well-ordered society should not regulate work and the workplace to treat everyone as free and equal.[82]

Now, according to interdependent independence, the normative disempowerment of the poor – their inability to legislate universally because an alien will *de facto* controls the conditions of their agency – also afflicts the worker subject to a capitalist boss. It does so, moreover, *whether or not the worker is poor*. One Kantian institutional remedy to this disempowerment might be to endow workers with the requisite public powers over their conditions of work, quite independently of rights to property. These may include a system of pro-labour labour law, but might also include more substantive public control over production. On this reading, Rawlsian property-owning democracy would be insufficient for Kantian independence. And now we find ourselves, again, further to the left of Toronto liberalism. In the next section, I will sketch a Kantian argument for public control over investment that supersedes both Kant's model of independent commodity production and Rawls' model of property-owning democracy. That argument tracks the influence of Kant's philosophy on the 'ethical socialism' of the late 19th and early 20th centuries.

I now summarize the argument of this section. According to interdependent independence, Kant's political economy of citizenship is not fundamentally about property and propertylessness, as the Toronto liberals argue. It is, rather, about control over labour capacity. I argued that such control is, in general, inconsistent with Public Right, unless it draws a special justification. One such

---

[81] The difference principle expresses Rawls's fraternity-type idea that benefits to the better-off are justified only if they benefit the worse-off as well. I discuss Rawls's account of fraternity in Section 4.

[82] Enfranchising powers and prerogatives under the difference principle would also allow self-esteem to come into play as a supplement to other maximinized primary goods, such as income and wealth. All this would tell in favour of something stronger than property-owning democracy, such as liberal socialism. I defend this conclusion in Vrousalis (2023, chapter 7).

justification, for Kant, is self-standing (*selbstständig*) production for a competitive market – that is, independent commodity production. Although independent commodity production is not possible under mechanized industry, Kant's normative theory, I argued, provides fruitful engagement with the topic of work that takes us beyond Toronto liberalism. In the next section, I explain how interdependent independence helps us make progress in contemporary political philosophy, by supporting a strictly egalitarian account of cooperative production.

4 From Independence to Economic Democracy

In Section 2, I argued for the interdependent independence reading of Kant's theory of citizenship. In Section 3, I argued that this reading is superior to the Toronto reading. In this section, I explain how interdependent independence provides a distinctly Kantian explanation for the injustice of socioeconomic inequality. Interdependent independence, in that sense, complements the burgeoning literature on the critique of inequality from John Rawls to Thomas Piketty. More precisely, this section discusses the economic presuppositions of a society of free and equal people – the supply-side of Right. I will raise a central puzzle from Rawls, discuss its criticism by G.A. Cohen, and offer a Kantian solution to it. My approach will be problem-led, as opposed to exegetical. If I am right, then Kant's political philosophy still has interesting things to tell us about the economic presuppositions of democratic citizenship.

4.1 Rawls' Ambiguity

According to John Rawls, the just society is a system of cooperation for mutual interest, in which citizens cooperate in reciprocally justifiable terms as free and equal. In this, Rawls follows a long tradition from Rousseau to Marx. Rawls discusses the kinds of justifications that can be offered on behalf of social and economic equality on the basis of his two principles of justice. These principles are supposed to reflect the three values of the French Revolution: *freedom* – reflected in Rawls' 'liberty principle' – *equality* – reflected in his 'fair equality of opportunity principle' – and *fraternity* – reflected in his 'difference principle' (Rawls 1971, 60 f).[83] Towards the end of *A Theory of Justice*, Rawls offers the following defence of the division of labour:

> a well-ordered society does not do away with the division of labor in the most general sense. To be sure, the worst aspects of this division can be surmounted: no one need be servilely dependent on others and made to choose

---

[83] A better term is *solidarity*, which does not depend on the masculine implication of fraternity. But I will stick to the original terminology to avoid confusion.

> between monotonous and routine occupations which are deadening to human thought and sensibility ... But even when work is meaningful for all, we cannot overcome, nor should we wish to, our dependence on others ... It is tempting to suppose that everyone might fully realize his powers and that some at least can become complete exemplars of humanity. But this is impossible. It is a feature of human sociability that we are by ourselves but parts of what we might be ... The division of labor is overcome not by each becoming complete in himself, but by willing and meaningful work within a just social union of social unions in which all can freely participate as they so incline. (Rawls 1971, 463)

Kant agrees with Rawls (and Marx) that the just society would preserve some form of the division of social labour.[84] I want to dwell on the positive argument of this passage, which focusses on meaningful work. 'Meaningful work' here stands for two things: first, work that is democratically self-directed in some strong sense and, second, work that involves sharing out arduous tasks or toil to such an extent that all workers have a reasonably equal chance of realizing themselves at work. Rawls' theory of justice proposes to buttress meaningful work through economic institutions reflecting the 'meaning of fraternity':

> The difference principle ... does seem to correspond to a natural meaning of fraternity: namely, to the idea of not wanting to have greater advantages unless this is to the benefit of others who are less well off. (Rawls 1971, 90)

Can this idea buttress Rawls' emphasis on 'meaningful work in free association with others'? The answer is not obvious, because fraternity, as Rawls elaborates it, rests on an important ambiguity. This is highlighted by the following example, due to G.A. Cohen:

> Two brothers, A and B, are at benefit levels 6 and 5, respectively, in New York, where they live. If they moved to Chicago, their levels would rise to 10 and 5.1, respectively. If they moved to Boston, they would rise to 8 and 7. Is fraternity, as Rawls means to characterize it, consistent with A proposing that they move to Chicago? If so, it is a thin thing. Or is Rawlsian fraternity strictly maximinizing? In that case, Boston is the choice, and in a feasible set with no bar to redistribution ... equality is the result. (Cohen 2008, 78)

By Rawls' own lights, just fraternity cannot be mere trickle-down from the privileged to the unprivileged.[85] To see why, suppose that being a banker or

---

[84] On Marx, see Kandiyali (2023).
[85] I will discuss two kinds of privilege: possession of productive assets that are *alienable* (like raw materials, factories, and physical wealth) and *in*alienable (like innate talent). 'Talent' here denotes an innate capacity that enables rent extraction. To clarify: what makes talent inequality potentially unjust is not the mere fact that Mozart has more talent that Salieri but rather the ability

singer offers a higher salary (or higher social esteem or is inherently more meaningful) than being a janitor. Schematically, the banker uses the market to leverage her savings, whereas the singer uses it to leverage her talents. Rawls asks: what kind of justification, if any, can the banker or singer offer to the janitor to elicit her productive contribution to their joint product, *given* that the janitor receives much less than the other two?

Whatever Rawls' actual response, a Chicago-type justification is unavailable to him. This is because Chicago, compared to Boston, only gives breadcrumbs to the janitor. It is therefore ineligible as an expression of Rawlsian fraternity. A Kantian reformulation of this thought could go something like this: if the private will of the privileged, as a whole, determines access to goods and services that the unprivileged need to be able to set and pursue their ends, then there is *pro tanto* an injustice.[86] I will elaborate on this Kantian twist in Section 4.3. Before I do, I must explain Cohen's critique of Rawls at greater length.

4.2 Cohen's Cut

Cohen (2008) attacks Rawlsian liberalism for its tolerance of inequality. Cohen insists that, since the owners of scarce productive assets in Rawlsian society will get more than non-owners, Rawlsian liberals are unjustifiably committed to 'giving to those who have' (Cohen 2008, 86).[87] He asks: what justifies the fact that the rich or talented will, in a Rawlsian society, fail to contribute the same amount of work at higher rates of taxation (for the benefit of the less well-off)? According to Cohen, such behaviour is normally unjust. The normality qualification is important, because a refusal to preserve output at a higher tax rate can be caused by an *unwillingness* to work as much or by the practical *impossibility* of doing so without impugning one's life projects. Sometimes the rich and talented *can't* maintain production at a higher tax rate – and that may be a perfectly good excuse – and sometimes they just *won't* maintain production.

To this distinction between 'can't' and 'won't', there correspond, roughly, two readings of the difference principle. The strict reading of the difference

---

of the former to extract rents from others, including Salieri. Under certain market conditions, talent is a scarce productive asset (much like land and machinery) enlisted as a source of profit.

[86] A background assumption here is that there can be no justification that a white male banker can offer to the non-white female banker for any relative benefit that tracks age, class, gender, or race. Inequalities traceable to such features are unjustified by Rawls's principle of fair equality of opportunity (Rawls 1971, 65f). The question is whether Rawls' difference principle can do more work than that, as his discussion of fraternity suggests it does.

[87] Cohen's emphasis here is on the owners of inalienable productive assets – the talented. But his argument applies equally to the owners of wealth who demand high returns in return for not relocating their assets abroad and/or who are willing to hire politicians to enforce that demand.

principle 'counts inequalities as necessary only when they are, strictly, necessary, that is, apart from people's chosen intentions':

> The lax reading, on the other hand, countenances intention-relative necessities as well. So, for example, if an inequality is needed to make the badly off better off but only given that talented producers operate as self-interested market maximizers, then that inequality is endorsed by the lax, but not by the strict, reading of the difference principle. (Cohen 2008, 69)

The lax difference principle entails 'giving to those who have', says Cohen. So we should favour the strict difference principle on justice grounds.[88] Put in terms of the Two Brothers case, suppose that A and B can rightfully coerce each other to go from New York to Boston or Chicago – as Rawls' theory of justice implies. Then they can rightfully coerce each other to go from New York to Boston, period. Chicago should not be on the cards. The argument for this conclusion goes as follows. According to the lax reading of the difference principle, the following argument is sound:

> Economic inequalities are justified when they make the worst off people materially better off. [Major, normative premise]
> When the top tax rate is 40 percent, (a) the talented rich produce more than they do when it is 60 percent, and (b) the worst off are, as a result, materially better off. [Minor, factual premiss]
> Therefore, the top tax should not be raised from 40 percent to 60 percent.

Cohen calls this the *incentives argument* for inequality. The incentives argument is an expression of the lax difference principle. According to Cohen, this argument has the same structure as the conditional threat proffered by a kidnapper to the kidnapped child's parents:

> Children should be with their parents. [Major, normative premise]
> Unless the kidnapper receives the ransom money, he will not return the child. [Minor, factual premiss]
> Therefore, the parents should pay the ransom money. (Cohen 2008, 39)

The two arguments are relevantly analogous, says Cohen, because both the rich and the kidnappers wrongfully demand rewards to which they are not

---

[88] Cohen thinks that social justice requires an egalitarian ethos in citizens, quite independently of justice in *public institutions*. Kantians will immediately raise their eyebrows here, charging Cohen with conflating *juridical* (extensionally individuated) with *ethical* (intentsionally individuated) obligations. But the lax/strict distinction goes through independently of the ethical. That is, the strict difference principle is a *normative standard* that mandates strict equality in the Two Brothers case, quite independently of whether it also requires an egalitarian ethos. So Cohen's argument can be made consistent with Kantian strictures about Right and Ethics, as long as the Boston distribution is in the feasible set and going to Boston (as opposed to Chicago) remains coercible.

independently entitled.[89] In a nutshell, Cohen's case against the lax difference principle is that it countenances incentive demands that are not reciprocally justifiable to free and equal people. The related Kantian thought, which never figures explicitly in Cohen's reasoning, is that incentive demands can never constitute an omnilateral justification for certain inequalities. Such demands are instances of might-makes-right, or attempts to return our social relations to the state of nature.[90] I now discuss this Kantian argument for the strict difference principle more closely.

4.3 A Kantian Argument for Strict Maximin

I began this section by asking what justification the banker can offer to the janitor either for earning more or for having a more meaningful job. According to Cohen, she can offer very little. And the little she *can* offer must be about what she *can't* do. Kant's political philosophy has a powerful argument for supporting this Cohenite conclusion. The argument is that 'won't'-type justifications on the part of the privileged are always invalid, because they are *attempts to make the direct producers into servants of the will and won't of privilege*. The idea is that, when the terms of social cooperation depend on the will and won't of privilege, none of us are free. So when the rich and talented say that they 'won't' keep up production when taxes are raised, they are not offering a genuine justification for not doing so. All they are offering is a conditional threat based on their collective might as owners of different kinds of productive assets.

Although Cohen never quite puts it in these terms, his analogy with the kidnapper suggests that he thinks of those who leverage their productive assets in the market in terms of such unilateral lawgiving. This does not mean that the privileged can, by right, be forced to work or to preserve their productivity. But it does mean that, *if* they decide to work, then they cannot use their market leverage to lessen their relative tax burden. So privilege is not wronged if it receives no incentives payments or if these payments are reduced or confiscated through taxation.

This Kantian argument from the independence of the worse-off has implications for how to think about economic power under capitalism. One of the major discoveries of Marx's critique of political economy was that capitalist control over productive assets confers on the capitalists control over the total stock of the labour capacities of workers. This control is consistent with capital and

---

[89] Note that such an entitlement cannot be grounded on desert or merit, because Rawls does not accept desert or merit as a ground.
[90] Contrast Chiara Cordelli's (2020) related Kantian argument against privatization.

labour being equal juridical subjects as commodity owners (of non-labour and labour inputs, respectively).[91] A corollary is the distinction between *market* and *economic* power. If markets are competitive, capitalists (individually and collectively) have no market power. But, at the same time, capitalists collectively *do* have a property-conferred economic power over the alien labour capacities of workers. In other words, capitalists collectively *can but won't* maintain their contribution to public institutions in response to a tax hike. More generally, the citizens' dependence for employment, social provision, production, and social reproduction, on the optimizing wills of the capitalists subjects the former to the constraining choices of the latter. This is why capitalism draws the same objection as poverty: in making the non-owners of productive assets into servants of capital, capitalism is inconsistent with the freedom of those non-owners. Cohen's argument is thus kantianized.

What are the relevant Kantian alternatives to capitalism? A relevant contrast is with an economic constitution in which the producers can use the stock of their labour capacities independently of privilege. Under independence, their use of these capacities is not subject to the will and won't of the owners of productive assets. On this reading, Kant's emphasis on *Selbstständigkeit* – the independent possession and use of one's rightful powers – contains in crux the democratic idea that the will and won't of privilege cannot figure in the justification of social institutions and their reproduction.[92]

I now return to Rawls. Although he does not address 'can't' and 'won't' directly, he does say that social and economic inequalities are justified only if

> The premiums earned by scarce natural talents ... are to cover the costs of training and to encourage the efforts of learning, as well as to direct ability to where it best furthers the common interest. (Rawls 1971, 274)[93]

This is an inchoate statement of the 'can't' and 'won't' distinction, indeed a concession to the strict reading of the difference principle. But the Kantian argument cannot stop here. It further requires that public power pick up the slack between 'can't' and 'won't'. That is, just as poverty alleviation must be provided by the state, so must the direction of overall investment. The reason is that only *public* power can attenuate the kind of discretion that capitalist private

---

[91] For the Kantian origins of this idea, see Section 3.3 above.
[92] You might wonder how a group of competing price-takers jointly constitutes a will. The answer is: salient groups can wrong other groups without necessarily being group *agents*. Certain pluralities, such as capitalists, polluters, men, white people, can have joint capacities, which is all that's required for them to 'will and won't' in the relevant sense. I discuss this in Vrousalis (2026).
[93] The burdens that Rawls says include the costs of training, incentives for learning, plus allocative efficiency.

Kant on Citizenship and Poverty 51

power has over the stock of our labour capacities. This remains true even under conditions of distributive justice and even if there are reasonable exit options to working for capitalists.[94] After all, the bare existence of these options does not preclude the domination of capital, unless these options are *up to* us in some strong sense.[95] What is 'up to us'?

Making the economy up to us could involve a combination of public control over alienable productive assets, together with high taxation over the use of inalienable assets. What form 'public control' should take cannot be settled here. But it would minimally require public ownership of major social utilities and credit institutions, as well as some form of planning of aggregate investment. In the interest of completeness, and for the sake of highlighting a broader point about structural domination under Kantian Right, I now sketch a well-known argument for this conclusion. My purpose is twofold. First, I want to show that influential socialist ideas have their roots in Kant's political philosophy. Second, I want to show how these ideas also illuminate the limits of his philosophy.

4.4 From Immanuel Kant to Eduard Bernstein

Outlining an argument dating back to the early days of social democracy, Przeworski (1985) explains how democratic governments under capitalism are structurally dependent on capital. The capitalists have power over governments in part because they can credibly threaten to disinvest, fire, relocate, or a combination thereof. Carrying out such threats will precipitate job losses and wage cuts, undermining any government's re-election prospects. Supposing that these threats are credible and that governments are interested in re-election, capitalists have structural power over governments.

But capital is not the only productive asset that can be leveraged in the market. As Cohen and others have shown, talent (and functionally equivalent inalienable assets) can be similarly leveraged. Suppose, *pace* Przeworski, that there is an economy of cooperatives, owned and controlled by their own talented workers.[96] Cooperatives, in general, are more conducive to equal freedom than capitalist firms, because they are unlikely to relocate in response to democratically authorized tax hikes, or to lay off workers in response to

---

[94] I defend this conclusion in Vrousalis (2023, 2026).
[95] Ripstein (2009, 2017) offers a masterful account of what it means to give ourselves laws under Kantian Right. But he does not realize that such self-legislation requires more than rule of law plus a generous welfare state. See Section 4.5.
[96] Perhaps the economy has the structure of Vanekian market socialism, in which loans from profit-seeking cooperative banks fund worker-controlled cooperatives (Vanek 1970).

minimum wage legislation, etc. These are the kinds of concerns animating democratic egalitarians, in general, but also Kantians, in particular.

Now note that, under a regime of private property in productive assets, these cooperatives must control their own investment, hiring, and pricing policy. There are, in general, two ways firms can affect voters and thereby leverage governments. They can cut worker incomes and they can increase unemployment. There are, in turn, two ways to increase unemployment: firms can lay workers off, or – assuming a growing labour force – they can fail to hire. Suppose that cooperatives are disinclined to fire their own members. They can still undermine democratic decisions by failing to hire new workers, or, less directly, by raising prices faster than nominal wages. Now suppose there is a democratically authorized decision to raise the minimum wage. Cooperatives can defeat this decision by threatening not to hire new workers. This 'won't' threat is, in turn, made credible by their failure to invest. For under a regime of private control over investment, 'the profits of enterprises today are the investments of tomorrow, and the investments of tomorrow are the employment of the day after' (Helmut Schmidt, cited in Przeworski 1985, 43). Private employment, in other words, presupposes private investment. It follows that the only way capital's threat can be made non-credible consists in wresting control over investment decisions from its private owners.

To sum up: private ownership of capital, whether by cooperatives or by capitalist firms, can only be reproduced by maintaining the owner's rate of profit. Maintaining profit sometimes requires higher unemployment and/or lower real incomes. Supposing that governments depend, for their re-election, on the overall level of unemployment, or of worker real incomes, and that private owners of capital control their own investment, hiring, and pricing policies, such owners will sometimes be disposed to wield power to the detriment of democratically authorized decisions. It follows that some form of public planning of investment may, for this reason, be indispensable to the enforcement of democratic authority.

How might we arrive at investment planning? Marx uses a familiar Kantian analogy to argue that capitalist private property begets its own gravediggers. The gravediggers are the capitalists themselves, who become obsolete once the division of labour develops to the point of separation between ownership and control. Marx writes: 'a musical conductor need in no way be the owner of the instruments in his orchestra, nor does it form part of his function as conductor that he should have any part in paying the 'wages' of the other musicians' (Marx 1991, 511). Once the joint stock company comes into the historical scene, the owner is no longer the manager. Therefore the functions of the capitalist can be separated from her ownership of productive instruments, just as the functions of the conductor can be separated from her ownership of musical instruments. It follows, says Marx, that *socialism* – the socialization of the means of production under a democratic state – is compatible with economic efficiency and a complex division of labour. Eduard Bernstein, one of Marx's literary executors, turned this idea into an argument for gradual approximation to socialism through parliament-led democratic reform.

Whether Kant would have endorsed such arguments is anyone's guess. But Bernstein's reformism did have a long *Kantian* pedigree. For the rest of this subsection, I explore two variants of Kantian socialism: ethical and juridical. Bernstein, for his part, took his reformism from the 19th century Neo-Kantians, especially Hermann Cohen.[97] Cohen offered a defence of 'ethical socialism' – a socialism founded not on Kant's *juridical* idea of external freedom but on his *ethical* idea of the Formula of Humanity.[98] Variants of that idea pervade the writings of Karl Vorländer, Lucien Goldmann, and the Austromarxists.[99] A boon for their theory seems to be that it unites ethics and economics, effectively subordinating the latter to the former.

Unlike the ethical interpretation, the juridical interpretation I presented above emphasizes cooperative production under a division of social labour. Kant's alertness to the possibility of the subjection of labour to property *despite* their formal equality as juridical subjects, his suspicion of large landownership and the concentration of property, and his commitment to state-led democratic solutions to these problems are all methodologically and substantively based on his juridical, non-ethical account of independence.

Now, a corollary of my interpretation is that these seminal ideas are unavailable if we focus solely on Kant's ethics. Therefore juridical socialism has considerable advantages over ethical socialism. I will mention four. First, Kant's juridical conception explicitly connects *labour* with free and equal citizenship, a move unavailable to his ethical theory as such. Second, his emphasis on property, contract, and status leads to a political economy of citizenship that foreshadows Marx's critique of it.[100] Juridical socialism therefore resonates with the critique

---

[97] On Cohen, See Widmer (2024). For the connections between Cohen, Jean Jaurès, and ethical socialism, see Ypi (2025).

[98] '*So act that you use humanity, whether in your own person or in the person of any other, always at the same time as an end, never merely as a means*' (*G* 4: 429). No one, to my knowledge, has studied the remarkable conceptual overlap between Hermann Cohen's late 19th century and G. A. Cohen's late 20th century ethical socialism.

[99] See Cohen (1902), Adler (1978), Goldmann (1968).

[100] Lucio Colletti (1970) argues that, since Hegel's theory of justice is essentially theological, Marx's secularization of Hegel is essentially a return to Kant. If my interpretation is correct, then one of the origins of Marx's critique of political economy is Kant's account of equal, commodity-producing, juridical subjects. So Colletti's conclusion goes through independently of his premiss.

of political economy (and related social science) in ways that ethical socialism does not. Third, juridical socialism does not presuppose any specific ethical or moral theory. It is therefore compatible with neutrality on controversial questions about the good life. Fourth, the focus on coercive obligations enables us to ask what free and equal people can rightfully coerce each other to do, quite independently of their ethical dispositions. By contrast, any socialist theory that begins by assuming away deep and pervasive ethical disagreement is assuming away politics. For all of these reasons, Kant's juridical theory of citizenship seems like a better starting point for rethinking the basics of the socialist tradition than his ethical theory. And whatever the starting point, Kant's influence on socialist thought is beyond dispute.

I now conclude by using this section's structural examples to highlight the structural limits of Kantian Right.

4.5 The Limits of Kantian Right

Kant's political philosophy offers a parsimonious and systematic framework for understanding the *externalization* of rightful relations between persons. Starting from an innate right to external freedom, through private right, we arrive at the rich diversity of the public institutions of modernity. In most cases, Kant proceeds deontically, by asking who wrongs whom and how. This is the private law model of litigants who require an impartial judge to give each her due. Perhaps predictably, this framework does less well dealing with *structural unfreedom*, that is, cases where the agency of either of the litigants is absent, mitigated, or intractable. Consider a Przeworskian illustration.

A newly elected government has a democratic mandate to raise taxes in order to build public roads. This mandate can be thwarted in one of two ways: through *corruption* and through *structural dependence*. Corruption involves the privileged (capitalists, landowners, the talented) bribing government officials not to raise taxes. Structural dependence, on the other hand, does not involve corruption. Rather, it operates on the type of mechanism explained in Section 4.4. For example, the privileged announce that, if taxes are raised, they will disinvest in the economy. Disinvestment means fewer jobs, unemployment, and eventually an outvoted government. So the government withdraws or waters down its democratically authorized plan.

Both cases involve a unilateral will thwarting democratic decisions. *But no agent or group exceeds their public mandate in the second case.* Indeed, in the second case the privileged are legally trying to maximize their rate of return, the voters are legally choosing the government that will create the most jobs, and the politicians are legally enforcing the will of the governed. Yet something goes awry; the political procedure is rigged in favour of the rich and powerful. Kant's political philosophy has intellectual resources for embracing this conclusion. In this section I have tried to mobilize some of them. But mobilizing them to the full means looking beyond the private law interpretation of Kant's theory of justice, whether in its Toronto variants or otherwise.

5 Conclusion

In this Element, I have presented an interpretation of Kant's theory of citizenship based on the idea of interdependent independence. On this interpretation, citizenship presupposes the ability of citizens to independently exercise their interdependent powers, including their productive powers. This, in turn, requires that they control their share of scarce productive assets. On this reading, no justification can be offered to the poor or the proletarians for being servants of the rich or of the capitalists, respectively. So poverty and wage-labour are not acceptable forms of social standing.

Looking at the bigger picture, Kant conceives of the modern state as a system of cooperative production, in which our reciprocal entitlements to one another's labour carry a justificatory burden. Like Rousseau, Kant offers an inchoate statement of what may be called the *labour theory of political obligation*. Political obligation, on this view, includes an obligation of juridical equals to contribute in proportion to their ability to the maintenance of the state, under conditions of labour independence. This explains why the empirical exemplary of Kant's citizen, implicit but ubiquitous in his political and anthropological writings, is the independent commodity producer under a republican state. Seen in this light, interdependent independence can explain Kant's disenfranchisement of women, wage labourers, and landless farmers, while making sense of all his examples and contrasts. Interdependent independence also anticipates Marx's discussion of commodity production by juridical equals, as well as his emphasis on unilateral control over alien labour capacity – *alienated labour*.

To sum up the argument of this Element: Kant's theory of citizenship takes the Enlightenment idea of equal juridical subjects one step further. Kant thinks of the modern state as a system of cooperative labour, in which our rightful reciprocal entitlements to one another's labour carry a justificatory burden. This is how Kant connects labour with citizenship. The downside is that a state legislating on behalf of economically dependent citizens would lack legitimacy. This is why he is wont to disenfranchise the poor. Yet Kant's obsolete distinction between active and passive citizens has a singular virtue: unlike contemporary liberal defences of the capitalist state, fidelity to Kant's own position need not pretend that the denizens of such a state can all be independent. For all its emphasis on inclusion, liberal capitalism presupposes that some of its citizens must remain dependent on the unilateral will of some ruling class – whether private owners of productive assets or unelected bosses and managers of these assets. In other words, the liberal capitalist state purchases inclusion at the cost of illegitimacy. The revolutionary implication is not to preserve the letter of Kant's argument through an indefensible exclusion of passive citizens. Rather, it consists in preserving the spirit of Kant's argument by guaranteeing all equal juridical subjects independent use of their interdependent productive powers: their independence in interdependence.

References

Adler, M. (1978). 'The Relation of Marxism to Classical German Philosophy'. In T. Bottomore and P. Goode (eds.) *Austro–Marxism*, 82–104. Oxford: Oxford University Press.

Allison, H. (2020). *Kant's Conception of Freedom*. Cambridge: Cambridge University Press.

Brosch, A (2024). *Haus, Markt, Staat. Ökonomie in Kants praktische Philosophie*. Berlin: De Gruyter.

Baynes, K. (1989). 'Kant on Property Rights and the Social Contract.' *The Monist*, 72, 433–453.

Cohen, G. A. (1983). 'The Structure of Proletarian Unfreedom'. *Philosophy and Public Affairs*, 12, 3–33.

Cohen, G. A. (1995). *Self-Ownership, Freedom, and Equality*. Cambridge: Cambridge University Press.

Cohen, G. A. (2008). *Rescuing Justice and Equality*. Cambridge, MA: Harvard University Press.

Cohen, H. (1902). *System der Philosophie, Erster Teil: Logik der reinen Erkenntnis*. Berlin: Bruno Cassirer.

Colletti, L. (1970). *Marxism and Hegel*. London: New Left Books.

Colletti, L. (1972). *From Rousseau to Lenin*. London: New Left Books.

Cordelli, C. (2020). *The Privatized State*. Princeton, NJ: Princeton University Press.

Davies, L. (2020). 'Active Citizenship and Kantian Republicanism'. In *Humanity and Personality in Kant*, 30–24. Berlin: Georg Olms Verlag.

Davies, L. (2021). 'Kant on Civil Self-Sufficiency'. *Archiv für Geschichte der Philosophie*. https://doi.org/10.1515/agph-2020-0030.

Dierksmeier, C. (2002). 'Kant on *Selbstandigkeit*'. *Netherlands Journal of Legal Philosophy*, 1, 49–63.

Dworkin, R. (2000). *Sovereign Virtue*. Cambridge, MA: Harvard University Press.

Essert, C. (2017). 'Property and Homelessness'. *Philosophy & Public Affairs*, 44, 266–295.

Flikschuh, K. (2021). 'Innate Right in Kant – A Critical Reading'. *European Journal of Philosophy*, 30, 1–17.

Fraser, N. (2023). 'Three Faces of Capitalist Labour'. https://criticaltheoryinberlin.de/en/benjamin_lectures/2022/. 11 February 2025.

Goldmann, L. (1968). "Is There a Marxist Sociology?" *International Socialism*, 34, 13–21.

Gregor, M. (1986). 'Kant Theory of Property'. *Review of Metaphysics*, 41, 757-787.

Guyer, P. (1996). *Kant and the Experience of Freedom*. Cambridge: Cambridge University Press.

Hardimon, M. (2009). *Hegel's Social Philosophy: The Project of Reconciliation*. Cambridge: Cambridge University Press.

Hasan, R. (2017). 'Freedom and Poverty in the Kantian State'. *European Journal of Philosophy*, 26, 911–931.

Hasan, R. and M. Stone. (2022). 'What is Provisional Right?' *The Philosophical Review*, 131, 51–98.

Hazareesingh, S. (2020). *Black Spartacus*. London: Allen Lane.

Hegel, G. W. F. (2015). *Hegel's Philosophy of Right*. E. Knox (ed.). Oxford: Oxford University Press.

Hodgson, L.-P. (2010). 'Kant on the Right to Freedom: A defence'. *Ethics*, 120, 791–819.

Holtman, S. (2004). 'Kantian Justice and Poverty Relief'. *Kant-Studien*, 95, 86–106.

Honneth, A. (2024). *The Working Sovereign*. London: Wiley.

Hruschka, J. (2004). 'The Permissive Law of Practical Reason in Kant's Metaphysics of Morals'. *Law and Philosophy*, 23, 45–72.

Hruschka, J. and S. Byrd. (2012). *Kant's Doctrine of Right: A Commentary*. Cambridge: Cambridge University Press.

Hussain, W. (2023). *Living with the Invisible Hand*. A. Ripstein and N. Vrousalis (eds.). Oxford: Oxford University Press.

Huber, J. (2022). *Kant's Grounded Cosmopolitanism*. Oxford: Oxford University Press.

James, D. (2015). 'Independence and Property in Kant's *Rechtslehre*'. *British Journal of the History of Philosophy*, 24, 302–322.

Julius, A. J. (2003) 'Basic Structure and the Value of Equality'. *Philosophy and Public Affairs*, 31, 321–351.

Kandiyali, J. (2023) 'The Importance of Others: Marx on Unalienated Production'. *Ethics*, 130, 555–587.

Kant, I. (1996a). *The Metaphysics of Morals*. In M. Gregor (trans.) *Practical Philosophy, 353–604*. Cambridge: Cambridge University Press.

Kant, I. (1996b). *Practical Philosophy*. M. Gregor (ed.). Cambridge: Cambridge University Press.

Kant, I. (1998). *Critique of Pure Reason*. A. W. Wood and P. Guyer (trans.). Cambridge: Cambridge University Press.

Kant, I. (2000). *Critique of the Power of Judgment*. E. Matthews and P. Guyer (trans.). Cambridge: Cambridge University Press.

Kant, I. (2013). *Anthropology, History, and Education*. R. B. Louden and G. Zoller (trans.). Cambridge: Cambridge University Press.

Kant, I. (2018). *Lectures and Drafts in Political Philosophy*. F. Rauscher and K. Westphal (trans.). Cambridge: Cambridge University Press.

Kisch, H. (1968). 'Prussian Mercantilism and the Rise of the Krefeld Silk Industry: Variations upon an Eighteenth-Century Theme'. *Transactions of the American Philosophical Society*, 58, 3–50.

Kleingeld, P. (1993). 'The Problematic Status of Gender-Neutral Language in the History of Philosophy: The Case of Kant'. *Philosophical Forum*, 24, 142–168.

James, D. (2016). 'Independence and Property in Kant's *Rechtslehre*.' *British Journal of the History of Philosophy*, 24, 302–322.

Loriaux, S. (2020). *Kant and Global Distributive Justice*. Cambridge: Cambridge University Press.

Ludwig, B. (2005). *Kant Rechtslehre. Kant Forschungen* 2. Hamburg: F. Meiner.

Maliks, R. (2014). *Kant's Politics in Context*. Oxford: Oxford University Press.

Marx, K. (1976). *Capital*. Vol. I. Harmondsworth: Penguin.

Marx, K. (1991). *Capital*. Vol. III. Harmondsworth: Penguin.

Marx, K. (1973). *Grundrisse*. Harmondsworth: Penguin.

McNulty, J. (2023). 'Class Struggle in the Rational State'. *British Journal of the History of Philosophy*, 31, 491–512.

Moran, K. (2021). 'Kant on Travelling Blacksmiths and Passive Citizenship'. *Kant-Studien*, 112, 1–22.

Nozick, R. (1974). *Anarchy, State and Utopia*. New York: Basic Books.

Pascoe, J. (2022). *Kant's Theory of Labour*. Cambridge: Cambridge University Press.

Patellis, I. (2013). 'Kant on Independence, Ideal and Empirical'. *Kant-Studien*, 104, 442–465.

Pinheiro Walla, A. (2020). 'Private Property and Territorial Rights'. In R. Demiray and A. Pinheiro Walla (eds.) *Reason, Normativity and Law: New Essays in Kantian Philosophy*, 1–28. University of Wales Press.

Przeworski, A. (1985). *Marxism and Social Democracy*. Cambridge: Cambridge University Press.

Rawls, J. (1971). *A Theory of Justice*. Oxford: Oxford University Press.

Rawls, J. (2001). *Justice as Fairness: A Restatement*. Oxford: Oxford University Press.

Ripstein, A. (2009). *Freedom and Force*. Cambridge, MA: Harvard University Press.

Ripstein, A. (2017). 'Embodied Free Beings under Public Law'. In S. Kisilevsky and M. J. Stone (eds.) *Freedom and Force: Essays on Kant's Legal Philosophy*, 160–210. Oxford: Hart.

Rousseau, J. J. (1973). *The Social Contract and the Discourses*. London: J.M. Dent.

Skinner, Q. (1997). *Liberty Before Liberalism*. Cambridge: Cambridge University Press.

Tierney, M. (2001). 'Kant on Property: The Problem of Permissive Law'. *Journal of the History of Ideas*, 62, 301–312.

Vanek. J. (1970). *The General Theory of Labour-Managed Market Economies*. Ithaca, NY: Cornell University Press.

Varden, H. (2016). 'Rawls. vs. Nozick vs. Kant on Domestic Economic Justice'. In *Kant and Social Policies*, 93–123. Cham: Palgrave Macmillan.

Vrousalis, N. (2015). *The Political Philosophy of G. A. Cohen*. London: Bloomsbury.

Vrousalis, N. (2022). 'Interdependent Independence: Civil Self-Sufficiency and Productive Community in Kant's Theory of Citizenship'. *Kantian Review*, 27, 443–460.

Vrousalis, N. (2023). *Exploitation as Domination: What Makes Capitalism Unjust*. Oxford: Oxford University Press.

Vrousalis, N. (2026). 'Walrasian Domination: Proletarian Unfreedom Under Perfect Competition, Exit Options, and Equal Political Influence'. *Oxford Studies in Political Philosophy*, (forthcoming).

Weinrib, E. (2003). 'Poverty and Property in Kant's System of Rights'. *Notre Dame Law Review*, 78, 795–828.

Weinrib, E. (1995). *The Idea of Private Law*. Oxford: Oxford University Press.

Weinrib, J. (2008). 'Kant on Citizenship and Universal Independence'. *Australian Journal of Legal Philosophy*, 33, 1–25.

Widmer, E. (2024). 'Hermann Cohen's Neo-Kantian Ethical Socialism'. *Kantian Review*, 29, 607–628.

Williams, H. (1983). *Kant's Political Philosophy*. London: St. Martin's Press.

Williams, H. (2006). 'Liberty, Equality, and Independence'. In G. Bird (ed.) *A Companion to Kant*, 365–384. Oxford: Blackwell.

Wood, A. W. (2005). *Kant*. Oxford: Blackwell.

Wood, A. W. (2014). *The Free Development of Each*. Oxford: Oxford University Press.

Ypi, L. (2014). 'A Permissive Theory of Territorial Rights'. *European Journal of Philosophy*, 22, 288–312.

Ypi, L. (2025). 'Kantian Socialism and the Critique of Technocratic Reason'. *Studi Kantiani*.

Acknowledgements

This Element reworks material previously published. Section 2 reworks my essay 'Interdependent Independence: Civil Self-Sufficiency and Productive Community in Kant's Theory of Citizenship' *Kantian Review* 27 (2022): 443–460. Section 3 is the revised text of my Marx and Philosophy Society Annual Lecture, presented in London in June 2023. Parts of it were published as 'Why Kant Is Sooner Socialist Than Toronto Liberal' in A. Kaufman (ed.) *Realizing Equality in Policy* (University of Michigan Press, 2025), 108–126. For helpful written comments on earlier drafts of the essays contained here, I would like to thank Micha Gläser, Rafeeq Hasan, Benjamin Hofmann, Alex Kaufman, Jan Kandiyali, AJ Julius, Pauline Kleingeld, Suzie Love, George Pavlakos, Igor Shoikhedbrod, Howard Williams, Allen Wood, and an anonymous reviewer from Cambridge University Press. For helpful discussion, I would also like to thank audiences in Amsterdam, Catania, Munich, London, Patras, Oslo, Rotterdam, and New Orleans. I must also record a debt to Arthur Ripstein, whose 2009 book *Force and Freedom* introduced me to Kant's powerful arguments for a social democratic state. My more anarchistically minded younger self would have greatly benefited from reading that book earlier than he did. This research was generously supported by the Netherlands Organization of Scientific Research (NWO) in the form of the Vidi grant 'Inequality against Freedom: Economic Power, Markets, and the Workplace' (016.Vidi.185.213). I also want to thank the NWO for paying for the Open Access license on this Element.

Cambridge Elements

The Philosophy of Immanuel Kant

Desmond Hogan
Princeton University

Desmond Hogan joined the philosophy department at Princeton in 2004. His interests include Kant, Leibniz and German rationalism, early modern philosophy, and questions about causation and freedom. Recent work includes 'Kant on the Foreknowledge of Contingent Truths', *Res Philosophica* 91(1) (2014); 'Kant's Theory of Divine and Secondary Causation', in Brandon Look (ed.) *Leibniz and Kant*, Oxford University Press (2021); 'Kant and the Character of Mathematical Inference', in Carl Posy and Ofra Rechter (eds.) *Kant's Philosophy of Mathematics Vol. I*, Cambridge University Press (2020).

Howard Williams
University of Cardiff

Howard Williams was appointed Honorary Distinguished Professor at the Department of Politics and International Relations, University of Cardiff in 2014. He is also Emeritus Professor in Political Theory at the Department of International Politics, Aberystwyth University, a member of the Coleg Cymraeg Cenedlaethol (Welsh-language national college) and a Fellow of the Learned Society of Wales. He is the author of *Marx* (1980); *Kant's Political Philosophy* (1983); *Concepts of Ideology* (1988); *Hegel, Heraclitus and Marx's Dialectic* (1989); *International Relations in Political Theory* (1992); *International Relations and the Limits of Political Theory* (1996); *Kant's Critique of Hobbes: Sovereignty and Cosmopolitanism* (2003); *Kant and the End of War* (2012) and is currently editor of the journal Kantian Review. He is writing a book on the Kantian legacy in political philosophy for a new series edited by Paul Guyer.

Allen Wood
Indiana University

Allen Wood is Ward W. and Priscilla B. Woods Professor Emeritus at Stanford University. He was a John S. Guggenheim Fellow at the Free University in Berlin, a National Endowment for the Humanities Fellow at the University of Bonn and Isaiah Berlin Visiting Professor at the University of Oxford. He is on the editorial board of eight philosophy journals, five book series and The Stanford Encyclopedia of Philosophy. Along with Paul Guyer, Professor Wood is co-editor of The Cambridge Edition of the Works of Immanuel Kant and translator of the Critique of Pure Reason. He is the author or editor of a number of other works, mainly on Kant, Hegel and Karl Marx. His most recently published books are *Fichte's Ethical Thought*, Oxford University Press (2016) and *Kant and Religion*, Cambridge University Press (2020). Wood is a member of the American Academy of Arts and Sciences.

About the Series

This Cambridge Elements series provides an extensive overview of Kant's philosophy and its impact upon philosophy and philosophers. Distinguished Kant specialists provide an up-to-date summary of the results of current research in their fields and give their own take on what they believe are the most significant debates influencing research, drawing original conclusions.

Cambridge Elements

The Philosophy of Immanuel Kant

Elements in the Series

Kant on Self-Control
Marijana Vujošević

Kant on Rational Sympathy
Benjamin Vilhauer

The Moral Foundation of Right
Paul Guyer

The Postulate of Public Right
Patrick Capps and Julian Rivers

Kant on the History and Development of Practical Reason
Olga Lenczewska

Kant's Ideas of Reason
Katharina T. Kraus

Kant on Marriage
Charlotte Sabourin

Kant and Teleology
Thomas Teufel

Kant on Social Suffering
Nuria Sánchez Madrid

Kant's Natural Philosophy
Marius Stan

Kant Incorporated
Garrath Williams

Kant on Citizenship and Poverty
Nicholas Vrousalis

A full series listing is available at: www.cambridge.org/EPIK

For EU product safety concerns, contact us at Calle de José Abascal, 56–1º,
28003 Madrid, Spain or eugpsr@cambridge.org.

www.ingramcontent.com/pod-product-compliance
Ingram Content Group UK Ltd.
Pitfield, Milton Keynes, MK11 3LW, UK
UKHW021859010326
468546UK00019B/788